PRAISE FOR
LEGACY

T0122641

I can't think of a better road map to scaling your legacy than this book. There is simplicity yet depth in the foolproof six Legacy Elements. LEGACY removes the daunting task of figuring out what levers can compound your time to accelerate results. As a reader, you will be equipped with a set of guiding principles to make your legacy bulletproof!

VERNE HARNISH

Founder, Entrepreneurs' Organization (EO)

Author, *Scaling Up* (Rockefeller Habits 2.0)

Marco has a deep passion for understanding what leadership is about. He has been highly dedicated in making himself and others achieve their best potential. It is through his personal experiences and desire to make this world a better place that this book was born. I am sure others will find inspiration and comfort from his story, his learnings, and the road map he has built from them.

CARTER MURRAY

FCB, Global CEO

It was 2,500 years ago, at his trial for asking the hard questions of those around him, that Socrates asserted that "the unexamined life isn't worth living." One hundred years later, his student, Aristotle, explored the concept of "the good life well lived." It's in this tradition that Gian Marco Palazio offers us his thoughts on legacy. It's so easy to merely exist—without purpose or intent. But, surely, we were put on this earth for a reason. A reason greater than ourselves. Gian Marco implores us to bring this thought to our daily interactions with those alongside us in our life's journey. That he does so with such humility, honesty, and vulnerability is what distinguishes him and this book from all the others. If only I'd had this book in my early years of marriage, fatherhood, and leadership ... in fact, it still resonates for me right now!

PETER A. REILING
The Aspen Institute

Each of us faces the daunting task of living the one unique life we've been given. How do we realize our full potential? Accomplish a work of significance? Love our families and neighbors and ourselves? Enjoy the journey and smell the roses? In LEGACY, Gian Marco gives us three things: a paradigm or set of glasses for looking at the issues in a fresh way, concrete examples from his own life that make the general principles clear and interesting, and practical suggestions and exercises. Your experience may differ from his, but I guarantee this will stimulate your thinking and inspire you to become a "Legacy Champion."

HARRY STRACHAN
Emeritus at INCAE Business School
Bain & Co. and Mesoamerica

Gian Marco Palazio is a true leader. This book will not only inspire you, but will also give you the blueprint to create a legacy that will transcend generations to come. His authenticity and his ability to create a simple, yet profound, framework makes this journey relatable to every man or woman who ever wanted to pursue greatness. Dive into this journey and get ready to find insights that can turn you into a great leader.

RAUL VILLACIS
Founder, The Next Level Experience

Legacy can be an intimidating topic. In LEGACY, *the reader will be challenged to pause and reflect on important questions in life while there is still time to make critical course adjustments. Gian Marco reveals, in a refreshingly honest way, his own journey to live a more intentional and meaningful life. He reminds us that our legacy begins now, not in some distant future.*

STACE LINDSAY
Advisor, Investor, and Educator

LEGACY

LEGACY

HOW LEADERS TRANSCEND THE PAST, BALANCE THE PRESENT, AND SERVE FOR GENERATIONS

G.M. PALAZIO

Advantage®

Published by Advantage, Charleston, South Carolina.
Member of Advantage Media Group.

ADVANTAGE is a registered trademark, and the Advantage colophon is a trademark of Advantage Media Group, Inc.

Printed in the United States of America.

10 9 8 7 6 5 4 3 2 1

ISBN: 978-1-59932-918-5
LCCN: 2018953200

Book design by Carly Blake.

This publication is designed to provide accurate and authoritative information in regard to the subject matter covered. It is sold with the understanding that the publisher is not engaged in rendering legal, accounting, or other professional services. If legal advice or other expert assistance is required, the services of a competent professional person should be sought.

Advantage Media Group is proud to be a part of the Tree Neutral® program. Tree Neutral offsets the number of trees consumed in the production and printing of this book by taking proactive steps such as planting trees in direct proportion to the number of trees used to print books. To learn more about Tree Neutral, please visit **www.treeneutral.com**.

Advantage Media Group is a publisher of business, self-improvement, and professional development books and online learning. We help entrepreneurs, business leaders, and professionals share their Stories, Passion, and Knowledge to help others Learn & Grow. Do you have a manuscript or book idea that you would like us to consider for publishing? Please visit **advantagefamily.com** or call **1.866.775.1696**.

I dedicate this book to my country of Nicaragua, wishing our people can learn from the legacies we have inherited and knowing we have the power to create the legacies we wish to leave our future generations.

AUTHOR'S NOTE

In the weeks leading up to publishing this book, my country of Nicaragua has been living a historic peaceful revolution, that unfortunately has taken with it some of a country's most valuable asset, its youth. The oppressive regime of Daniel Ortega has stolen in cold blood over 350 lives and injured thousands.

This is a collective crisis engulfing a whole nation that was sparked overnight and forever will be remembered starting on April 18, 2018. The new normal in our country has us suffering economically and still battling a regime that avoids admitting to any wrongdoing. While this could take months to solve, and possibly many lives more, we are looking for a peaceful transition and praying that those in power realize the opportunity they have to create a legacy based on the few rescuable values they may have left.

In *LEGACY*, we touch on the legacy of ancestors and even that of an entire country. The cost to repeating history is so expensive and completely unnecessary. I invite everyone interested in creating a legacy worth examining to remember this fact and that we are more than capable of breaking any historical or inherited legacies that are not worth repeating. With such palpable examples of negative legacies in front of us, it is more urgent than ever to have this in our top of mind and to work to create, rule, and expand a worthy legacy with intention every day.

TABLE OF CONTENTS

INTRODUCTION
LEGACY CHAMPIONS

Every day I build my legacy with clarity and intention and it is indestructible!

During your last breaths, when you consider the legacy you have left on the world, are you going to be fulfilled with no regrets? Will you be leaving your family and organizations with material abundance to keep building on your life's work? Will you be secure in your spiritual connection? Will you have lived your legacy to your fullest potential during your lifetime?

Before we answer those questions, let's answer two questions fundamental to understanding this book: What is a legacy? And what is a legacy champion?

A legacy in the truest sense is defined as the structure, support, and future that you leave behind to enrich your family, friends, and community.

A legacy champion is someone who works toward their own self-betterment and self-actualization purely for the sake of making the world a better place for those who will inherit their community, lives, and spiritual space. This is someone who consciously transcends their past, balances their present, and serves for future generations.

A legacy champion isn't a glory-filled role—it requires a lot of work, true sacrifice, and an evolving need for self-betterment that comes from true awareness. If you're on the path to become a legacy champion, be aware that often you won't be the first to get your needs met. You may sometimes be the last. But your lack of selfishness will pave the way for a better version of yourself for everyone around you.

When it comes to legacy, our goal is to create a journey so rich and impactful that when our last day comes, there will be no regrets. With awareness, we can evolve past our faults, failures, and mistakes, by building a stronger foundation for our future as a legacy champion. By the end of this book, you will know legacy is something you can create, rule, and expand in every part of your life, for the benefit of you and those you share it with.

This book is written for entrepreneurs who want to expand their success by embracing awareness throughout all facets of their lives, so they can enrich their futures. For both men and women who want to honor their personal values and spiritual practices in order to form a baseline awareness to intentionally move forward with their legacy for the rest of their lives.

THIS BOOK IS FOR YOU.

This book is written for those looking to overcome obstacles in their lives, whether personally or professionally, to form a better awareness and a better sense of self that is needed to become a legacy champion. This book is written for entrepreneurs who want to expand their success by embracing awareness throughout all facets of their lives, so they can enrich their futures. For both men and women who want to honor their personal values and spiritual practices in order to form a baseline awareness to intentionally move forward with their legacy for the rest of their lives.

Within the work of becoming a legacy champion, there are six Legacy Elements that, when fully understood, form the basis of our legacy experience within **The Legacy Element System**: love, energy, grounded reality, abundance, connection to source, and you. Each element of Legacy integrates all other elements. For example, if we focus on love, the five remaining elements have a direct impact on all of the love spheres of your life.

This book is intended to be an initial guide to creating, ruling, and expanding your legacy. Told through stories from my past, as well as delving into the underlying awareness that I have gained through those life experiences, I will show you how you can begin the journey of becoming a legacy champion. At the end of each Element of Legacy chapter, there will be a series of challenges that, when engaged with while reading the material, will transform your understanding of becoming a legacy champion, as well as put you several steps forward towards achieving your goals. It's in your hands to envision and manifest your legacy, that's your unique power that rests within you. We all have untapped capacity, so why not begin to expand your legacy today?

> It's in your hands to envision and manifest your legacy, that's your unique power that rests within you.

ACTIVATING THE SIX LEGACY ELEMENTS

To help us understand such a B-I-G idea as legacy, I use six Legacy Elements to guide you forward through the path to become a legacy champion. To see the path in each chapter, you'll need to take an objective look at every area of your life through the lens of growing your legacy and take positive, forward thinking steps to enhance each specific area from smallest to largest. We can move forward by using small, intentional shifts and using our awareness of what needs to change to create an indestructible legacy.

These six elements work together, acting as a system of checks and balances that we can utilize to make sure our lives are in harmony as it relates to being a legacy champion. By being intentional with each element, we can bring about serious change to our legacy throughout every area of our lives.

FIRST, WE MUST ESTABLISH THE MEANING OF EACH LETTER IN THE LEGACY ELEMENT SYSTEM:

L **Love.** If we never love ourselves, we will never be able to give love. If we don't give love in our lives, we won't receive love and if we don't have love in our lives we will never be complete. Our deepest fears are rooted in a lack of love.

E **Energy.** We must have energy and health in our physical bodies to have the capacity for everything else in our lives. We must have energy and clarity in our mind, so we can strengthen our emotional fitness and stamina in order to give our relationships the very best of ourselves. Energy is frequency and we must raise that frequency by feeding off others and aligning ourselves with their resonating frequencies.

G **Grounded Reality.** We must be grounded in our current realities which will tell us the path of action we need to take to get to where we want to be in our futures. Being grounded every day keeps us working our hardest because we know we have a limited time on Earth. We have a sense of urgency about what we're going to do with that time.

A   **Abundance.** Abundance is a mind-set and a divine energy we need to create to be a legacy champion. It is the result of our hard work and material abundance supplies you with an external confidence. Abundance gives us freedom to fulfill our desires, choose options, and execute on opportunities. We are never dealt more than we can handle in our pain or in our abundance.

C   **Connection to Source.** This connection is our default programming with the Source that we have covered up with a bunch of malware in our everyday lives. It's our base support system and the voice that speaks to us when we're quiet enough to listen to it. Connection is our inner peace and true happiness, our safe and cozy space that gives us an internal certainty and sense of knowing that we're never alone. Deep connection with our Source is the ultimate legacy.

Y   **You.** You must understand yourself over anybody else, rule yourself over anybody else, and humbly be yourself over anybody else. Fulfill yourself. Align with yourself. Celebrate yourself. Love yourself. Be at peace with yourself. Refine yourself. Never stop learning about yourself.

> Never stop learning about yourself.

CREATE, RULE, EXPAND.

We gauge ourselves on a daily basis mentally, physically, emotionally, and spiritually, so that we can empty our brain and fill it with intentional thoughts. Without our everyday awareness, we can't serve ourselves or anyone else to the best of our abilities. We can't spell the word "legacy" without every letter present. So, if we're omitting or ignoring one of the elements, then legacy is not being

If we're omitting or ignoring one of the elements, then legacy is not being created, ruled, or expanded.

created, ruled, or expanded.

While our processes for shaping what content fills our minds each morning is different, we need to acknowledge our basic mental, spiritual, emotional, and physical needs every day to be our best selves. We do this to remain aligned with all aspects of the Legacy Elements System. If we're misaligned, then we're unable to perform at our full capacity, so we must undertake the conscious choice to build a better understanding of ourselves and realign our elements.

In order to keep ourselves in line with the best of our intentions, we have to stay knowledgeable and aware of our obstacles. Obstacles serve as feedback to teach us where we need to grow in our lives, and give us the intuitive push to go to another level in order to overcome them. If we ignore them, rather than putting them to use, then we're doing ourselves a disservice.

A solid process isn't dependent on your Legacy Elements always being balanced, but only that you're aligned within your element integration. That's the most important piece of the puzzle. So, for example, you can have an imbalance at work that's affecting your abundance element. However, you will eventually align yourself if you attend to every other element in your life, because, over time, working on your other elements will improve your work challenges because your mind-set will shift. As abundance overflows from integrating the other elements, your work life will become easier when everything else is flowing at a fuller capacity.

When you raise your awareness, you can work wonders on the future of your legacy, entering into a mind, body, and soul pact that only builds and strengthens with time. By making intentional choices, any possible worries, doubts, or fears become obsolete. Once your intentions for your future become more defined, you're able to push away any negative emotions. You have a clearer understanding of where you need to go attain the life you want for yourself and for your legacy. This momentum snowballs into a growing awareness and acts as an inspiration and guiding light to yourself and others. By honing your internal focus to create the life you have always dreamed of, you can orchestrate a better life for those who will come after you.

MY LEGACY CHAMPION JOURNEY

In 2012, during a week-long meditation retreat in India, my mistakes, failures, accomplishments, and my future life's path were clarified to me during intense meditation sessions. For the first time, I was able to take my entire time on this planet up to that point and deep dive into it. I was really getting in tune with the Voice of what I consider the Source, or my Creator, God. I was primed to begin to receive a more conscious connection to the Voice of Source.

I realized I consciously began my personal development journey to becoming a legacy champion after being heartbroken back in college. The breakup could have been avoided had I been more aware of the situation, took ownership for my lack of awareness, and owned my pain. This awareness followed me after I graduated, as I upended my way of life and moved back to my native Nicaragua in Central America. The move forced me to be alone with my thoughts, my doubts, and my pains until I became comfortable with, and even craving, my alone time to allow space for these internal movements. The only way to move forward through the opportunity of a new life and environment was by consciously moving through an active growth and development process. I kept pushing forward in life with an internal itch to search for growth, guidance, and eventually a more refined purpose.

I've had a lot of pain and shame throughout my journey, but recognizing these negative emotions has led me to learn more and empower myself, both internally and externally, to become the best possible version of myself.

This itch eventually transformed into a heavy pull, which transformed into a process of self-discovery that took me through the hallways of loss, pain, growth, and maturity that continues today. Since then, I've had a lot of pain and shame throughout my journey, but recognizing these negative emotions has led me to learn more and empower myself, both internally and externally, to become the best possible version of myself.

My entrepreneurial adventures began at age twenty-one, in the second poorest economy in the Americas, undercapitalized and with little infrastructure and market to build on. Because of my eclectic experience as a serial entrepreneur with multiple successes and multiple failures in the challenging business environment of Central America, I've gained a wealth of entrepreneurial knowledge that's worth sharing with others.

I'm thrilled to expose myself to share my story because I know there's value in being vulnerable. One of the most valuable lessons we can learn, which greatly increases our capacity for leadership, is to remain open, honest, and comfortable with our individual journeys.

Today, I do my best to execute as a legacy champion, someone who consciously works within their limitations to maximize their potential in every Legacy Element by being conscious and intentional with his life choices. This requires daily recognition of the power of heightened awareness and life affirming choices. As a committed investor to my own personal development, who has invested over twenty years and hundreds of thousands of dollars into full immersion programs, I've developed a passion for legacy creation as well as empowering entrepreneurs with the tools needed to mold their futures.

My life as a legacy champion isn't strictly related to my business ventures. In order to embrace and shape your legacy, you have to refine your awareness in all areas of your life, in every role you play. Through twelve years of marriage and three children, ages seven through ten, my intimate relationships have had their struggles. But I've been actively and intentionally tending to my marriage, which has gone from being potentially at its breaking point to a passionate, supportive relationship full of communication and mutual respect. From my renewed relationship with my partner to becoming a highly invested and present father, pushing each day toward a brighter future is paramount to my awareness.

After overcoming being thirty-plus pounds overweight and not taking care of my body by smoking and drinking to excess, I've come to respect my vessel by living a healthy, active lifestyle. Respect spreads through every area of my life including my eclectic spiritual experiences. As well as through the philosophy shifts that have pushed me to scratch the surface of my ultimate potential and keep going forward as my own champion day-by-day, year-by-year.

LIVING WITH LEGACY AWARENESS

Living with legacy awareness requires a commitment and consistency that most would consider crazy or unreasonable. But becoming a legacy champion is an urgent mission. That's both the point and the catch. To truly scratch the surface of our potential, we have to become intentionally unreasonable with sub-standards in each area of our lives. Our adherence becomes a legacy lifestyle choice in order to transcend the past to create your legacy, balance the present to rule your legacy, and serve future generations by expanding your legacy.

As we begin to move forward and expand our capacity by raising our standards for living, people around us will see the transformation within us. As our internal awareness grows, our external choices will also change and those around us will sit up and take notice of these shifts. However, the external changes in our lives will not happen until we have first made the internal changes within ourselves. This is why we must learn to build awareness throughout our everyday lives that can expand our ability for self-change including keeping the importance of our six Legacy Elements in the forefront of our minds. When we work from the Legacy Elements, there is little room left for wavering toward our ultimate goal of leaving the planet a brighter and stronger place after we've left it.

The external changes in our lives will not happen until we have first made the internal changes within ourselves.

CHAPTER ONE
LEGACY ELEMENT OF LOVE

Is love worth rescuing? For sure there is
a relationship, business, health condition
or spiritual connection worth rescuing
today. Make your decision now!

My wife has had "the talk" with me—the dreaded conversation relating to how I wasn't living up to our marital expectations—on dozens of occasions during our first years of marriage. Our conversation would inevitably start with a gentle sit down while I watched TV, or rested in bed. My wife would normally start off our conversation with a statement similar to:

"Listen, I got worried last night. I think you drank too much, said things that I didn't like and did things you shouldn't have done."

Unfortunately for our relationship, I got this speech quite frequently. As a social guy who's used to unwinding after a hard week at work with a few drinks among friends, I was unable to see how my priorities were skewed. Weekend nights I stayed up late and my wife went to bed without me. Unable to see the impact it was having on my relationship, I kept making the same careless mistakes because they felt good to me. Needless to say, this didn't always mesh well with my wife's wishes.

Honestly, this was a time of freedom. I convinced myself that my work ethic during the week as an entrepreneur would grant me a pass in explaining myself to anyone, or so I thought. I felt like my time was mine after work and during the weekend. Why should I explain myself during my time when I was being responsible and taking care of us? Meanwhile, my wife watched me having a good time from the sidelines, or she pretended to be bored so I would leave with her for the night. Unable to see her actions as clear communication of her unhappiness, instead I saw her as a drag. Bachelorhood was ingrained in my social ways and selfish behavior. I wasn't used to balancing the emotional expectations of someone else. Now that I was the man of the house, she needed to adjust to how things were going to be in our lives. Right?

Of course, this expectation on my part forged a lack of communication in our relationship that soon became a huge barrier between us. Our lack of common language, defined as a communication skillset where both parties can better understand what the other is saying with a heightened awareness using mutually agreed upon and understandable terms, wasn't very sustainable.

It got to a point where all I wanted to do was go out without my wife and catch a ride back home with someone else. Or even better, have the get together at my house so I could stay up until dawn and she could go to sleep whenever she wanted without bothering me. My lifestyle started to take a physical toll on my health and on our marriage. We both sought help in the first year of our marriage from different sources, and she became what I considered to be depressed. To me, it seemed as if she was giving up on us. We were arguing all the time. I couldn't figure out why she was being a quitter when it came to the problems in our relationship. I felt as if she were giving up on our marriage without a second thought, which didn't improve our situation. We were at an impasse with both of us privately considering throwing in the towel.

Eventually, I started finding answers by going through leadership programs, learning, maturing, and getting myself together. But I wasn't happy with purely being on the path myself, I wanted my wife and I to learn and grow together. At night I regaled her with knowledge from my various leadership and entrepreneurial seminars and gave her all my program materials. I pushed her onto the same path I was following, only she didn't need my pressure. By throwing my leadership pamphlets in her face, I wasn't communicating in a productive way because I was making her resent me for forcing her into a place of change, especially with her three pregnancies in our first years of marriage. She wasn't ready for the process and forcing her into *my* process wasn't making our situation better. I needed to help myself first, go down my own path, and then maybe she could find her path and react better to me once I'd made a change within myself.

> I needed to help myself first, go down my own path, and then maybe she could find her path and react better to me once I'd made a change within myself.

This is only a summary of some of the challenges during our first years of marriage. This chapter is a culmination of our pitfalls and the resulting tricks that we picked up to avoid making the same mistakes twice throughout our successful partnership. By helping myself first on the path to becoming a better entrepreneur and family man, I was able to mold what I've learned to my professional and personal life. While working through the Love Legacy Element we must be mindful that at its core, this element comes from the selfless changes within us, both toward ourselves as well as others. The Love Legacy Element can be defined as the act of selfless love, both for yourself and those around you, by prioritizing seven steps to maintain balance within your present that will allow you to lead with love in the future to build a strong legacy foundation.

Love is the first of the six Legacy Elements because any path on this earth must be started with love as the first step. Especially while becoming a legacy champion, one must become selfless with their love to truly be prepared for the process as it's a key element to having the right outlook for legacy creation. It also strengthens core relationships both with yourself and those around you, which can solidify relationships needed for support in the future.

As our relationship has progressed, we have trusted in seven key strategies to develop our Love Legacy Element.

Love Legacy Elements

1. Common Vocabulary

2. Forgiveness and Flexibility

3. Polarity

4. Presence

5. Priority

6. Leverage the Bond

7. Transcending Selfishness

1. COMMON VOCABULARY

What really brought us together again was when we developed a common vocabulary between us. We started growing together and worked really hard at it. Once you begin to identify and name the various moments, habits, and reference points of your relationship so you can develop a common language, it elevates your communication so you're less likely to engage in common misunderstandings.

A large percentage of the arguments with my wife were about our differences in our definitions of things. Something as basic as:

"I'll be there in five minutes."

"Is there enough money in the account?"

"Go ahead."

Simple conversations were often misconstrued between us. We didn't understand each other completely because our life experiences, expectations, and ways of being were different. Until it became clear to me that the more we learned about ourselves and the more we built a common language, the better our communication skills would grow over time.

Common language can come into play during critical moments when there is stress building between us and one of us mentions a common term. I once wrote my wife a letter explaining to her that within me, the king of our kingdom, lives "Snake Eyes," the warrior who comes out to save the king or kingdom when they are threatened, this includes threats by her! I detailed how much the king wants to honor, serve, and love the queen (her) and let her know that Snake Eyes is always on call and is quite an efficient warrior. In times of escalation where I feel I'm being cornered I gently remind her Snake Eyes is being woken up. That playful term can recharge the moment with humor or act as a deflection so friction doesn't escalate. These intentionally aware, basic, and even stupid, jabs and reminders at each other give us a chance to build a relationship based on awareness, respect, and fun, rather than feeding into unnecessary insults and vicious cycles.

On a cumulative basis, a lack of authentic interest in your mate is what leads to a poor relationship. I can honestly say that few relationship victories have felt so good than those earned by giving my partner the ugly truth due to our common language. Simple, and possibly stressful, miscommunications are avoided by having the same emotional language and definitions. These can come from education we have learned together at seminars like reminding ourselves of the Five Love Languages,[1] Six Basic Human Needs,[2] and others I refer to later in the book.

By using common terms with each other, you can stay on even ground with healthy communication and decrease the likelihood of turmoil by defusing complicated emotional situations. When you're not aware in your relationships, you will have easy emotional buttons to press, which could cause defensiveness or conflict. The less you're aware, the more exposed your buttons are to be pushed by your significant other when they aren't necessarily trying to push them. The more aware you are, your buttons become less exposed and harder to activate without thinking about your significant other's original intentions.

Before my wife and I shared our common language, we would often get into communication trouble while driving out to the beach to spend the weekend with our family. During the two-hour drive she would comment or ask about a work subject of mine. She had the best intentions, the information, knowledge, and interest to

---

1   Gary D. Chapman, *The Five Love Languages: How to Express Heartfelt Commitment to Your Mate* (Bhopal, India: Manjul, 2010).
2   Tony Robbins, "Tony Robbins: 6 Basic Needs That Make Us Tick." *Entrepreneur*, accessed May 31, 2018, https://www.entrepreneur.com/article/240441.

help and contribute, but the manner in which she would deliver her comments would trigger me to a near immediate flash point. I would see her commentary as an attack or insult.

Though it wasn't so much her words as her inflections, her tone, and what I assumed to be her "I can't believe you haven't done this" attitude with regards to my business. I couldn't overlook her perceived attitude or my anger. But as I grew to understand her point of view and learned to control myself, it was easier for me to take her well-intentioned comments and for her to also deliver them differently in a language that worked for me.

Learning how to communicate with each other is just as important as knowing what to say to each other. In a relationship, delivery of your communication is more important than the communication itself. That's how you build a stable emotional platform and a partnership in order to maintain a healthy legacy with your significant other by your side.

2. FORGIVENESS AND FLEXIBILITY

When I was less aware, my wife would consistently barrage me with questions about work. The common denominator underneath all her comments was good intentions. Since it's lonely at the top for the most of us, we make most of the decisions on our own without outside intervention. When those decisions are later questioned, and the positive results we anticipated aren't there, we already feel guilty. We're ashamed. We're fearful of the results—and mostly the criticism because the promise behind our actions didn't meet up to our expectations.

When those decisions are later questioned, and the positive results we anticipated aren't there, we already feel guilty.

When our partners notice our fear, and they launch into us with questions or comments, no matter how well meant their intentions, it goes against our ego. It goes against the fact that they're not slaying entrepreneurial dragons every day, so what do they know? We don't see their good intentions and because of our lack of awareness, we immediately react which results in an escalating argument that could have been avoided. Soon the pattern becomes a vicious cycle. It wasn't even the exact words she said to me. It was her delivery, expression, and non-verbal communication.

After a couple of years of this pattern between my wife and I, our resentment was piling up. I continued to barricade myself in my fortress, avoiding conversations with my wife, and playing defense. This obviously affected our relationship as well as our intimacy.

But as I grew more self-aware, I found that I wasn't breathing during our arguments. I was often short of breath and didn't breathe deeply enough so oxygen could reach my diaphragm. By not getting enough oxygen into my lungs, I wasn't taking the down time that I needed to assess our arguments before I furthered the conflict between us.

So, I actively started breathing during our escalating conversations to take the time I needed to process her intentions. I would take in her questions, not respond, breathe, and be aware. Then I would slowly remind myself her questions were asked with good intentions and that she had a point. By then I would be able to respond in a peaceful manner. *The change happened within me.* As a result of my shift in awareness, a shift happened within her too, because she saw that I was able to change my reaction.

I was able to forgive my wife because her intentions became clearer due to my awareness. I began appreciating our conversations that previously sparked tension. By changing my tactics and being more flexible, I was able to cultivate new communication abilities to relate to my wife. Obviously, I had asked her to change her delivery multiple times in the past, but the change had to happen in me for our communication to thrive. This change included cultivating my forgiveness and gratitude for having her support, instead of taking our relationship for granted again.

3. POLARITY

When my wife and I started growing together, we identified that we both have multiple personalities inside of us, so we started naming them. These "personalities" are parts of ourselves that don't normally come to the forefront unless we were under pressure or stress. When her anger would show up, we would both understand it was "Molly" talking, and not my wife. Then I would say something similar to:

"Oh okay, hello Molly. I didn't know you were joining us for dinner!"

This little comment introduced levity into an otherwise possibly tense situation. We would move on and laugh instead of taking her mood shift personally and thinking she was a crazy woman who would be one person in the morning and another in the afternoon. It's not only my wife with the split personalities either, she knows I have a darkness inside of me that can destroy anything either with my words or my anger.

My wife is an engineer, super practical, and very methodical in her thinking. While I have a good balance of analytical and creative mind-sets, I'm mostly creative. So those times when she turns into the ultimate engineer, it really turns me off. She goes toe-to-toe with me on my decision-making and strategy, which feels like she's undermining my abilities. She's smart, so I want her input, but sometimes her strong analytical and engineering qualities go overboard, and her energy feels masculine to me. If we're both in our masculine energies, we'll butt heads and turn off the polarity of the masculine vs. feminine. This polarity drives the passion in any relationship.

Likewise, sometimes we go out on a date night and leave the house without knowing where we want to go on our date. I ask her, and she says wherever. I say wherever, too. We're both in our relaxed and fluid states where nobody is taking control. Again, we clash. We clash because neither of us are taking a masculine leadership role and we're both in free-flowing feminine energy. I end up driving to five different places until I inevitably get mad and finally make a decision. If I would've made a choice in the first place, there would have been no problem. For men and women to have passion, there needs to be opposite energies and a polarity created by both the masculine and feminine. We must balance each other out so both energies are represented at all times, otherwise the lack of duality will create unnecessary conflict.

4. PRESENCE

We maximize our legacy by treating the women in our lives with patience, trust, thoughtfulness, and respect. Men are very direct in not only their energy, but their way of thinking. They pretty much ask what's the problem, how can I solve it, and what needs to be done for these results to happen in a focused manner. Men think much more efficiently with actionable items, both work-wise and results-wise. We're very action-oriented. Which means we don't take much time to sit with our emotions or be in an actively present state of mind. Conflicts become clear cut and issues are resolved without much emotional involvement.

When they consistently doubt their situation or don't have external confidence, or internal certainty within themselves or in their surroundings, women feel everything and their minds are a tornado of emotion. When they are communicating, and feeling all these emotions, it fills them up with doubt. However, it's a lot easier for them to make and maintain vulnerable connections on a relationship level than most men. Women require a feeling of safety and security in their relationship, and it's a precursor for physical touch. It's very important for a woman to have a feeling of safety before she advances in her relationship, even if she's married and has been married for years.

For example, if my wife has had a flustered day when I come home from work, she'll need me to give her my undivided attention for at least ten or fifteen minutes, so she can vent and get her mind re-centered for the rest of her day. I've learned that merely trying to fix her problems doesn't work for her at all. She needs me to be thoughtfully present and there for her emotionally.

So, I'll sit there and get the brunt of her emotional storm. Then when I see her shoulders come down and she breathes a little bit more, I'll know she's more tranquil. I can come closer to her and maybe kiss her, caress her, and then ultimately be intimate without her being internally troubled or distracted by her emotions.

I also know if I come home from a trip after I've been gone for five days and I immediately want intimacy, she's going to be like, "I don't care if I've been married to you for twelve years. Who *are* you?" Because we need to reestablish our emotional connection and she needs me to show up for her, so we can reconnect. So she can feel safe and secure to vent any emotions she's been holding back since I've been gone. She needs her space to be heard. That's the way women communicate, through their words. While most of us men prefer silence, grunts, noises and pointing. By being present in a communicative safe space for my wife, I can establish and strengthen our connection, which only builds on our existing loving relationship.

5. PRIORITY

Marriage is a marketing campaign. So, you need to practice KYC, Know Your (most important) Client, which is your wife. She's your most important client in life because she's your biggest supporter and your partner through all of life's challenges. When your kids grow up and leave the nest, the only people that are left are you and your significant other, which can be startling to two people who aren't on the same wavelength in their relationship. Many divorces happen during this stage.

If your energy goes everywhere else but into your marriage, there will be a disconnection. And if this accumulates, the need to reposition ourselves is paramount. You must survey your client and know if she thinks your partnership is working together or not and, if not, how to fix those issues together. Where are you bringing more value to her knowledge, her emotions, her safety, and her sense of security?

One year I decided to make an intentional change in the way my wife perceived our relationship by actively being grateful for my wife. I gave her a gratitude journal that I'd written for forty days, writing down two reasons a day why I was grateful to have her in my life. I packaged it nicely and gave it to her on her birthday and it was her favorite present! Because of the way I started consistently appreciating her through my gratitude, I began treating her differently. Our relationship shifted to another level because I actively decided to look at her, as well as us, differently.

It's important to understand what your wife or significant other wants in terms of her love language. If you haven't read *The Five Love Languages* by Gary Chapman, I highly recommended you do, to learn ways to establish how you and your partner both like to give and receive love, so you feel emotionally taken care of in a relationship. I think when I learned the essential Five Love Languages it was so much easier to satisfy my wife because we spoke the same language and were better able to communicate. Her love language is quality time and mine is physical touch. Paying attention to your significant other as your best client requires even more work and more attention than your best client at the office. Having the clarity on how to prioritize my wife through quality time made life so much easier for me—and happier for the both of us.

6. LEVERAGE THE BOND

When you've embarked on a lifetime commitment with this one person, you're going to go through multiple relationship stages during your lifetime. You're going to go through the honeymoon stage, adaptation stage, pregnancy stage, early parenthood, child-focused stage, empty nest, and golden years stage.

Relationships face constant metamorphosis over time, so you need to know what she wants in all areas of her life, whether that's her own physical body, how she feels loved and cared for, or something as simple as understanding her food preferences. As well as what she's willing or not willing to do, and if you're willing to share that space in her life.

For example, I work out every day. My wife goes maybe three times a week. She doesn't like to do the majority of exercises that I do because of some past injuries, so we rarely exercise together. However, there are other couples that have an entire relationship built around their exercise routines. They're willing to share the space they have in common together because their relationship can thrive in that area.

Another common relationship area to build on together is spirituality. How can I understand my wife's spirituality? She's a very devout Catholic. Now I'm also a Catholic, but I don't consider myself very religious. But in the last few years, we've started going to church together as a family every week with much more consistency. Whereas before I would weasel my way out of going to church as often as possible, now I'm one of the promoters of going to church with my family. What does that give my wife? That gives her stability and peace of mind.

We have a mutual family vision that it's important for our children to have a baseline understanding of our religion as well as a complete religious experience while growing up. If they choose to go another direction when they get older, that's fine, but for now they're going to have a quality Catholic experience. Which means going to church and going through all the different processes that being a Catholic requires. That's where I yield to my wife, to meet her expectations of happiness and our combined philosophy for our children's religious experience.

This common area bonding process in your relationship also involves upgrading yourself, so you have more capacity to give to your significant other. It's what energy you're going to bring and what willingness you're going to have to make sure that she's satisfied in all these areas. How can you prepare yourself to serve her needs and make her happy?

7. TRANSCENDING SELFISHNESS

From my personal experience, for the first three or four years of my marriage it was still all about me. I was still living like a single guy. My wife was waiting for me at home, and whatever was left over energy wise from my long day was hers, which obviously wasn't enough. I wasn't honoring my relationship or my wife by treating our bond this way; instead I was driving a wedge between us with my lack of service in her honor. My thought pattern and bad habits needed to shift so I could prioritize the energy focus on the most important areas in my life.

Treating your significant other like your best client involves consistently marketing and innovating to her needs within your relationship. That includes refining and developing your skills as well as your capacity to deliver her needs, your capacity to be present, and your capacity to satisfy any new needs that might arise, because relationships are consistently changing. This is a work in progress that means you must ultimately tend to your needs as well as your partner's needs so you can repeat the cycle without facing emotional burnout.

The biggest destructor of capital in the world is divorce, now running at a rate of 56 percent in the US, purely because of the expense and the destruction of previously existing unified plans. So, if your significant other isn't your first priority, they're going to let you know, whether directly through communication or by their actions. It's your responsibility to check for those sometimes not so significant signs of discontent, because most people have no problem changing a problematic situation for an easier, happier one.

Everyone's always looking for the BBD, or the bigger, better deal. If you don't have your number one client prioritized, they're going to find a bigger, better deal. You can look at it as they'll find a hobby, she'll find attention, or a sense of importance from someone else. So while you're three- or four-timing your wife with work or hobbies, even though you're not being unfaithful to her physically, you're not prioritizing her with your energy and your presence.

Energy and presence is much more important than physical intimacy because it's without selfishness. I can be on a trip, and my wife will know if she's still a priority. I've gone on trips where she's a total priority and I'm always in communication. Or I've gone on trips where she only gets one important communication during the day, but she feels the importance of my energy and my presence. There will also be trips where she's not a priority and I'll come home to someone who feels abandoned. I try not to let those happen very often by keeping my awareness open and working for me.

My wife will absolutely let it be known that she feels as if I'm neglecting her emotionally or physically. You can take finding the bigger, better deal to whatever extreme you want to take it, but it's definitely playing chicken with your legacy in a negative, risky way. Especially when it comes to your family's integrity, your happiness, your ability to contribute to a relationship, and your finances. Because the more separation there is between a couple, the more expensive it becomes in the long run.

When you're working as a team, you're both willing to be flexible to support the whole. But when you're feeling abandoned, you're going to find the leftover resources in the relationship, and many times that's money, to fill that void. Whether it's a man with his toys, whether it's a woman with her outfits. Then eventually that leads to divorce, and there's nothing more expensive than divorce. By maintaining these seven areas of awareness in your relationship, you can maximize the strength of your relationship's foundation which in turn makes your legacy that much stronger as you look toward the future together and any possible conflicts.

CHALLENGES TO THE READER

You can share this legacy journey with your spouse or significant other, but the one who has to do the work is you. They can change, because you change. They can react to you, because you've acted. But it all starts with *your* awareness as well as building yourself up to better serve your relationship. I've outlined several examples of intentional, legacy defining choices to strengthen your marriage from a daily, weekly, monthly, and yearly perspective below, so you can gather a better understanding of how to create a solid foundation for your legacy.

DAILY:

- Be the first person to say good morning with a hug and kiss as well as saying goodbye and wishing them a wonderful day.

- Get used to saying, "I love you." There are moments where it's said lightly and there are moments where it can be felt between you. If the words are never said, you will never know which instance is most meaningful and worth a memory.

- Chat throughout the day and be playful, funny, and sexy.

- Share at least one meal together.

- Give each other a minimum of fifteen minutes of pure presence by listening and accepting their daily verbal dump.

- Never go to bed mad.

- Pray together.

- Give your significant other compliments.

WEEKLY:

- Go on a weekly date night. Get out of the house together for dedicated alone time to serve your significant other, make them feel important and like your number one priority.

- Go somewhere together, that's not necessarily a date, something out of your regular routine and you will develop a sense of teamwork.

- Celebrate your business wins and discuss your challenges

together. Our partners will give us insights that can shine new perspectives on situations.

MONTHLY:

- Spend a weekend somewhere either with or without your family.

- Come clean with your spouse about how you're feeling and be vulnerable. It's rare that a man opens up, so when we do our partner feels very connected to us and can better understand us.

- Have a mystery date.

- Work on a family project together.

- Ask each other to grade your relationship as a whole from one to ten. If it's not a ten, what's missing between you to reach that number?

YEARLY:

- Plan a couple's honeymoon trip in addition to an anniversary trip. If your finances can't cover both vacations, you can combine these two trips. Some partners understand mixing a romantic trip with a day of work or a work meeting, but many want 100 percent of your dedication focused on them. This means they are your full priority and everything else can wait until you get home.

- Before planning the trip, get your hands on your significant other's bucket list as well as your own to compare them. Make sure there is a surprise or mystery element that you've planned for them during your trips. They'll appreciate the thoughtful gesture and that you went the extra mile to please them.

- If you travel a lot for work, spell out your quarterly travel plans with them before you leave. That way they feel confident and in control of knowing where you're going to be while they're at home.

- Align your philosophies for the enterprise with those for your family and make sure you have the same vision for your futures. Make sure you're going in an aligned direction together. The worst feeling is thinking your partner wants to go in another direction with important family matters when you're on another side of the fence.

- Find a couples retreat and learn together. It can be at your church, a local entrepreneurial organization, or with a relationship coach. It's important to discover the details and psychology of relationships together so you can create a baseline for your own working relationship.

- Do an annual budget and family investment plan for any home additions, car acquisitions, and anything else they can get excited for in the future.

- Write a gratitude journal listing all the reasons why you're grateful they're in your life. Write in it twice daily with two separate reasons you're grateful for thirty to forty days in a row. You'll quickly see how your shift in how you view them changes the way they act toward you. Package and deliver it as a surprise on a special occasion.

- Do something that stretches you and makes you a little uncomfortable, like a public act of love. Make them laugh with you, as well as at you, during your grand gesture.

HOW THE ELEMENTS OF LEGACY INTEGRATE INTO LOVE

ENERGY

To be able to give love we must develop strong love energy within ourselves. First this entails having physical energy and mental stamina to have leftover energy for those around us. Enough that not only gets us through the day, but that allows us to come home refreshed to our families after slaying dragons all day. Love energy requires presence, focus, and openness as well as active listening, which is key within strong love energy. This also involves asking revealing questions and allowing your loved ones to reach their own conclusions, instead of pushing your points of view on them.

GROUNDED

In relationships it's important to be realistic and sometimes allow our own self-interests to take a backseat in the interest of our loved ones. This is where our service, attention, and dedication need to be put into perspective to match up to the relationship goals we plan to grow and maintain with our loved ones. Which also means we can't have time for everyone. For our mental sanity, we must make sacrifices with our time. Remember, our women want attention all the time. Our kids want our attention for hours at a time. Our dear friends and extended family will also require time to maintain their relationships. How do we juggle all of these expectations on our time? Let's be realistic.

Let's design our schedules around key time investments during the day, week, month, and year. For example, each of my kids gets an international, father-child dedicated trip for four to five days. However, realistically, I can only provide this time allotment for my children once every two years because of resources, scheduling, and because I have three children! So, each child, every six years, will get a special trip with me for quality time. I also know that if I haven't visited my mother in three to five weeks, I'm long overdue. I need to give her a visit of three to four hours of 100 percent dedication, for her sake and for mine. My wife, on the other hand, requires a minimum of fifteen to twenty minutes of my full presence during our conversation per day to feel that we're connected. **Know which relationships are your priority and invest wisely in them.**

ABUNDANCE

Could you ever run out of love for your spouse, children, mother, or best friend? It's a weird question, but you might have that problem. **When it comes to love, this is where we should be an overwhelming and infinite geyser for the people in our lives.** There's probably not anything I appreciate more than traveling as a family to a new land, discovering new things, and learning together. Although I feel I could do this with my family for an unlimited amount of time, it's not realistic. But my abundance of the willingness to do so will never run out.

There isn't any amount of hugs and kisses I could give to my loved ones and say, that's enough. Why? Because that abundance of energy is pure love, infinite within my soul for everything that's important in my life and is one of the closest feelings to being God-like that I can think of in the world. So how am I going to run out of love abundance unless I'm misaligned out of this mind-set? As people prefer to be overdressed for occasions, I prefer to over love on every occasion.

CONNECTION

As previously mentioned, **when giving love, it's close to a God-like state.** Simply because that's the way God loves us, so we're experiencing Divine nature. When we're conscious about this, then we're in gratitude, we're abundant, we're full of energy, and we're connected as people, as one. When love is given in this state, words are unnecessary and can even spoil the moment. Because so much is said when we align ourselves with our Divine love presence.

YOU

Before we give love, we must love being ourselves. **We must love ourselves, forgive ourselves, celebrate ourselves, and care for ourselves.** Your vessel is your responsibility and if your mind-set, energy, and alignment are off, then the love you give will come at a deep cost for the ones you care for every day. That's why self-work is the most important area that will give you the most leverage in a well-lived life and expanding your legacy.

CHAPTER TWO
LEGACY ELEMENT OF ENERGY

When you are stuck, look back and
remember that your past obstacles,
challenges, and pain are what formed you
into the amazing person you are today!

The word "energy" carries many different meanings and definitions, whether we're relating it to either physical, emotional, or spiritual energy. However, all three interpretations involve maintaining balance as well as utilizing each energy to maximize our output on a daily basis. How you access these energies typically depends on your mental or spiritual development level, and your current life stage. Either way, each of the three energies are important and serve a purpose toward our greater good. It's only when we start to understand and work within our energies that we can mold and expand our energy levels to better suit ourselves, as well as our day-to-day existence.

For those entrepreneurial readers who have demanding schedules, physical energy is a key component to get through the day. This includes exercising consistently and being in shape. Without our body's help and health, we can't maintain the mental or physical strain of a certain pace or lifestyle. By maintaining our physical energy to its highest peak potential, our efforts prepare us for any other imbalances within our other energy centers, including emotional and spiritual, that might be thrown our way.

For instance, when we're carrying the burden of heavy, emotional energy as a result of a conflict with a loved one or friend, the negativity drags you down and creates an imbalance between your spiritual and physical energy. This type of toxic energy can plague all the other energy areas, until we're empty of all excess energy. Releasing the drama from our lives allows us to emotionally, physically, and spiritually recharge, and invest in healthy emotional energy again.

Nothing brings power and energetic certainty more than finding deep spiritual peace. By tapping into peace and spiritual energy, being mindful of that balance reminds us that we're infinite, energetic beings, which helps propel us forward through life. By cultivating our spiritual energy, we're expanding our certainty and keeping our series of energy checks and balances in place in case anything comes along to rock the boat.

By aligning these three energy centers and by building consistent awareness and personal practices to develop them, our dedication will give us the fountain of legacy youth we need to expand our legacy every day.

By aligning these three energy centers and by building consistent awareness and personal practices to develop them, our dedication will give us the fountain of legacy youth we need to expand our legacy every day. Nurturing these three energetic centers is required if we want to expand our legacy to become the champion that's needed for those around you and your world to flourish for the future.

AN ENERGETIC AWAKENING

In early 2017, I was facing off against one of the biggest professional challenges of my life and making some extremely tough choices to contract my main business. A lot of negative energy was going into fixing my problems. In every area, my energy seemed to be draining away from me. While at the same time, I was also the Chapter Chair for YPO in Nicaragua, which is the most influential business organization worldwide, with more than twenty-five thousand global members. While being a positive influence in my life, it also required a lot of energy resources that weren't necessarily available because of the heavy problems I was facing within my business. Each of these aspects of my life took a great toll of energy, until a lot of myself was split in two trying to juggle it all. It was an innate dichotomy between carrying the burden of my business failures, and devoting a large chunk of my energetic tank to leading other leaders. In a way, coming to terms with both sides of myself took the most energy out of me, and left me with little resources to replenish the balance.

That spring I had a world-class, international event to put together and host at my home while also balancing several other business stressors in my day-to-day life, which depleted a lot of my leftover energy and unbalanced my energy scales. During that event, Sifu Rama, a Chi-Kung master who had dedicated his life to studying his craft, was staying with us as our special guest and facilitator for the weekend. For those unfamiliar with the ancient Chinese practice, Chi-Kung is a holistic set of movement postures and exercises that feed into meditation, as well as controlled breathing, to encourage a calmer mind-set—rebalancing and redistributing our physical and mental energies through awareness.

His energy was peaceful, especially for me since I had so much on my mind at the time. In our moments of one-on-one conversation, I had the opportunity to ask him multiple questions about energy, balance, and life. Although I never showed anything overtly, I'm sure, as a master of understanding emotional presence, he understood how to read my energy. He was probably picking up on the amount of stress and mental baggage that was stuck on my shoulders trying to balance multiple roles in my life.

After the event when I dropped Sifu Rama off at the airport, what I felt through his energy was that I didn't need to worry about the stressful burden on my shoulders. He assured me, through his warm eyes and hug, as would a deeply understanding father, that I had the capacity to continue on with my life and create whatever I had the desire to create without boundaries. We shared a moment of communication and understanding without words at the airport curb. From that moment, I carried that clarity and knowledge that without worry, my energy was limitless within myself. It was a moment of peace and surrender when I had been carrying an infinite amount of stress and self-inflicted weight that was zapping my energy sources. It was, simply put, a spiritual moment.

What I found as a result of juggling my chaos was that by sticking to my rituals that reenergized me and maintained my focus, day-in and day-out, the energy I devoted to those rituals helped me structure my attitude when it came to facing my challenges.

What I found as a result of juggling my chaos was that by sticking to my rituals that reenergized me and maintained my focus, day-in and day-out, the energy I devoted to those rituals helped me structure my attitude when it came to facing my challenges. I was able to keep myself on track by dialing into daily rituals, which raised the awareness levels of my energy. This, in turn, allowed me to do my best work, which helped the event go smoothly. Because of my ability to articulate and understand my goals (as well as my awareness of what needed to be done when I stepped back from the overall vision) the event went beautifully, and everyone was very pleased with it.

Energetically, this experience was a release of tension, but my greater understanding of how my energy ebbs and flows has since added immensely to my spiritual energy practice. I now carry within me a certainty that if I remain constant in my energy rituals and replenishing myself, there's nothing I can't take on in my future. The emotional energy I created by giving myself the permission to surrender to my feelings was a huge uplifting breakthrough, as well as the idea that I held the power to shape my energetic reality without tearing myself apart to be everything to everyone. Our limits fall away when we work to maintain the balance of our energies and understand that we can keep that balance, while allowing ourselves to take a step back from time to time.

Energy Legacy Elements

1. Awareness.

2. Grow your impact while leveraging your energetic centers.

3. Be the co-creator of your own destiny.

1. AWARENESS: WHAT IS AND ISN'T SERVING YOU ENERGETICALLY

A legacy can be shattered if one element in our lives is not attended to regularly or isn't up to par with our other elements. We must constantly build awareness so that the elements that make up our legacy are up to our standard. Our awareness should grow in line with our capacities, so we can constantly be moving forward and making educated decisions that work toward our desired legacy. We are more impactful when we are aware in how we're handling our energy, as well as what energy we're giving out to others through both negative and positive situations. Our situational awareness within our legacy elements gives us a better understanding of our impact on others today and for the future.

For instance, in order to become a legacy champion, I had to form an awareness and acceptance of where I was in my life in order to change and evolve into my best self. A large part of that process occurred for me when I opened myself up to meditation. I found my own philosophy to take stock of my life and what needed to shift in order to make the future stronger for those I loved, as well as myself.

An empowering breakthrough came when I was in Fiji at a Tony Robbins event. It was during an exercise in the Life Mastery course where we were supposed to write down an addiction or habit that was not useful to our bodies. I sat down with my partner and it just hit me why I smoked, a habit that was detrimental to both my physical and emotional health.

My father smoked during the entire twenty-four years he was in my life. He constantly cheated multiple heart attacks, coming out of them not only laughing, but also smoking again. After five heart attacks with only 18 percent of his heart functioning he was forced into a quadruple bypass open-heart surgery. A month later, at seventy-three, he passed away. Even though he had the genes to make it into his nineties, his health choices had finally caught up to him. I was twenty-four when he passed. Although he played chicken with his mortality, I honor him for living life on his own terms, as selfish, naïve, and damaging as they were in the end.

Ever since I started partying in college, I would drink and liked being the last one awake with my cigarette because it provided me with moments to reminisce. Reminiscence is something of great value to me and drives me energetically on an emotional level. I would look at the night sky and enjoy a cigarette while I nursed the last drink of the night remembering the good times and blessings in my life.

Many times, the thick smoke enveloping me would transport me to a time when my father was alive, or remind me of being in his presence. It was a moment of connection. Between the pungent smell and misty curl of smoke, memories were my connection to him. The man whose love I craved, whose acceptance was always there, but whose recognition was difficult to gain. He showed me what discipline and work ethic looked like, molded my love for nature, and lived a full life experiencing the world.

However, sitting with my awareness back in Fiji with my partner doing the exercise, it became so clear to me that I wasn't going to follow in my father's footsteps. He had given me a gift. The pain of an example of what not to do with my life. Many times, that warning was more valuable and clear-cut than what I should do with my life, because I realized useful boundaries within creating my legacy.

I realized smoking was my subconscious connection to him. Only I came to understand, in a moment of clarity, that I could connect to him at any time. I could speak to him and share my feelings and ask his advice anywhere without having to smoke or drink to accomplish a connection. My connection with my father had officially become ethereal, spiritual, and most importantly, timeless. Available whenever I wanted it. That realization was a significant breakthrough and a conscious decision to change the way I related to my memories of him. In a split second, I was able to connect the underlying subconscious need for an emotional, sentimental connection with my father that was driven by the repetitive physical addiction of smoking.

Smoking wasn't serving me well in the long-term; it threatened my health, and thus my legacy. By stacking these bases and forming a self-awareness, it allowed me to create an example of massive change in any area of my life. After nineteen years of smoking, I'm cigarette free more than six years later and more connected with my father's spirit than ever before. Thank you, Dad!

2. GROW YOUR IMPACT WHILE LEVERAGING YOUR ENERGETIC CENTERS.

This book calls on you, the entrepreneurial reader, to find your own legacy champion philosophy. It serves as a reflection of where we come from and where we'll go as both men and entrepreneurs as long as we accept that our every action has a consequence that ripples through our lives—including the example we leave behind when we're gone. Intentional awareness comes with a conscious switch that you can flip to accept responsibility in creating your life, embracing gratitude through your grounded reality, and an understanding that you're capable of creating your own greatness through the choices you make with the time you have left on the planet. However, none of this will be possible without proper energy alignment and development.

Here are five ways to develop your energetic centers so you can leverage your legacy and create more impact:

1. Return to your center.
2. Stir what you love and celebrate.
3. Beware of ego.
4. Start a resetting ritual.
5. Align passions and purpose.

RETURN TO CENTER

Coming back to your center can be as simple as putting on some headphones, closing your eyes, and listening to a song during your lunchbreak. Or quiet meditation and reflection by taking a moment to sit in your car and become present in your body through breath, touch, or stretching. Our ability to get back into alignment with our bodies and our physical selves through breath and meditation gets us out of our heads.

Our minds are the biggest double-edged sword in the universe. On one hand, it's where our focus, creativity and analytical brain power stems and where we begin to manifest our realities. On the other, our minds are our biggest critic and stores all our doubts, pains, shames, and fears. Both functions are necessary and coexist, because without darkness, there is no light. So instead of letting the darkness take over, recognize it and appreciate its value.

STIR WHAT YOU LOVE AND CELEBRATE

As a good bartender, we should practice stirring our favorite drink. Find the ingredients, put them together, stir, and enjoy. By finding the things in life that we absolutely love, it's an easy way to get back to ourselves. That could be a phone call to your significant other, focusing on a picture of your children or reminiscing about a great moment that you shared with your parents. One of the greatest abilities we have as humans is to be able to transport ourselves using our mind to re-create an entire environment with emotions and feelings of that moment. By using our mind, we're using our best ability to transport ourselves out of a moment of stress to another place where there is peace. Transporting ourselves to moments we cherish is a great, everyday opportunity to form an awareness of our emotional, physical, spiritual, and psychological difficulties so that we can overcome them.

I find myself stirred with my family in nature or on a trip discovering a new land. My connection to nature is important and I know it moves my essence. When I see my children running, playing, and laughing on the beach, I quietly hold my wife's hand and we know it's a picture-perfect moment. Another gratitude selfie stamped on my heart. I'm also stirred by winning with my business team, celebrating a success that has cost us effort, sacrifice, and the alignment of our team. This is what makes being away from home worthwhile.

It's so easy for us to list all the negative things in our lives, or the have-nots. However, making a list of victories can be challenging. The problem is we're focused on what we aren't or haven't achieved yet. Instead, I have learned to celebrate nearly everything instead of the negativity. The more we condition ourselves to celebrate, the more momentum we have for positivity in our lives. By giving all our energy to celebrating the little things, our attitude will change our outlook and our energy. This will create a winning attitude and momentum. Nothing is more attractive than success. Developing the habit of winning is key for our legacy to endure because the habit breeds positive energy that in turn breeds positive expectations. Others feel this and want to be surrounded by winners.

BEWARE OF EGO

While embracing our awareness of self, we must also acknowledge the negative power of our ego and how that impacts our intentions for our legacy. Obviously, you won't have attained any level of success without being competitive and wanting to finish first. It's a natural human condition. But I think that as we start having success in the external world by being recognized, congratulated and sought after, our ego gets inflated because we start affixing titles to both our identities and ourselves.

We become the "leader," the "successful entrepreneur," and the "provider." The guy who handles hundreds to thousands of employees whose livelihoods rest on his shoulders. When the money rolls in and you can throw cash at problems, this becomes not only a defense mechanism, but also an eventual crutch for your self-worth. For the most part, people revere and feel pressure to become their titles and perceived identities in the world. That's what enflames egos and makes them grow.

But when those adopted identities start being questioned and start collapsing, you start doubting yourself. That doubt turns into guilt for not living up to that identity, which then turns into shame. Shame shifts into fear. From fear we can either go one of two ways: We can give into those dark energies by taking our fear out on our family by sedating ourselves with drugs, alcohol, or any other number of distractions that we can find on any digital device or ultra-niche tribe out there. Or we can turn that fear into fuel by transforming our negative energy into productive energy. This positive productive energy comes through awareness. It can become a source of nearly unlimited supply of energy for massive action to improve the reality of our situation. Also gained in the process is massive wisdom as we go forward toward the future.

What I found during my process is that when you go through these dark emotions of guilt, shame, fear, and doubt, you're putting all the pressure on yourself. You think the world is judging you, but your biggest judger is you. We can learn to love ourselves, and we need to do more of it. We need to forgive ourselves and give ourselves a chance. You know what? For the most part, the world won't even notice our faults or shortcomings.

External changes in our lives will not happen until we have made the internal change within ourselves.

People around us will only see the transformation within us because the things on the outside will start changing because of our emotional awareness. External changes in our lives will not happen until we have made the internal change within ourselves. Then things start changing, our energy changes, and we allow life to flow a little bit better and smoother.

START A RESETTING RITUAL

Once we've mastered our egos and have sat with our sense of self, another way to gauge our capacity is by putting into practice what I like to call the Resetting the Table Ritual.

A lot of my experience has been in the restaurant business. My last internship in college was at a global fast food corporate office. I opened and had to close a popular local franchise, and today our full-service coffee chain has over ten stores. We serve people every day. One of the best life examples from the restaurant industry is that we're all servers in life. Those that provide the best service to others without expecting much in return are the ones that are the most successful. How does this apply to our own lives? How does this apply to legacy?

First, we must set our table because no one can eat well at a table that isn't set with utensils, plates, and glassware. This involves setting our intentions for the day in the morning and becoming aligned to serve, that way we can bring our best selves to the table during the rest of our day serving others. We can easily tell during the course of a day who hasn't taken the time to reset their table that morning because they are in misalignment, in a bad mood, or lashing out in some negative capacity through their words or actions.

As observers, we naturally want to stay away from those people with messy tables mainly because we know we aren't going to receive good service from the person who isn't ready to serve. Whereas people who are constantly ready to serve and mentally reset their table, offer details and nuances within the experience that offer the others being served a way to capture a memory that can create a legacy.

An echo of the scripture in Psalm 23:5: "Thou preparest a table before me in the presence of mine enemies; thou anointest my head with oil; my cup runneth over."[3] This completely describes the Resetting the Table Ritual because as I set my table, I'm prepared to encounter my darkness and disempowering actions during the day, but I walk and serve those misaligned people and distractions with my best self and God given gifts.

How can we reset our table and provide the best service every day as leaders, parents, and entrepreneurs? Resetting the table means preparing myself for the day and the possible customer interactions I'm about to have, even though I have no idea who will show up or what type of day they've had before they meet me. We execute the resetting ritual to get us in the right mind-set before we interact with anyone. The resetting ritual can take as little as thirty minutes or as long as two hours depending on your personal tailoring, but what matters is that we do it with intention and do it every day. The desired result of resetting the table is to be able to serve those that

---

3   Ps. 23:5 (KJV).

come to us with the very best intention of service, while maintaining our energy and focus and executing to the best of our ability.

My resetting ritual looks like this every morning:

As I wake up in the morning, the first thing I do is drink a large glass of water with my vitamins for the day. Then I go to the restroom and release all the toxins acquired during the evening, get dressed, and drink my vegetable juice or green drink. These drinks help clean out my system, keep me regular, and alkalinize my system, as well as contribute valuable nutrients into my body.

I prefer to start my resetting ritual with two songs of meditation and this can last anywhere between five to twelve minutes. It's my time to quiet my mind, having recently woken up, and not allow noise to disturb my thoughts. During this time, I empty the cup of my mind and allow the Voice of Source to connect with me. The understanding that we were put here for a higher purpose, a higher process, and a higher legacy is the reason we dedicate time and respect to connect to the Source. This meditation allows me to listen and drives my actions derived from a series of closely followed orders by me for that day. For example, if an idea comes to me, I write it down and act on it. Whatever actions I may be reminded of in that moment are deemed important, as menial as they are, and I act on them immediately. If an idea flows into my head for content, I immediately send it to get shared on social media. There is no discussion, filters, but especially no doubt or fear. I pay attention to the Voice and act on it with complete trust.

Then I play a song for my gratitude. This is where I shower myself with gratitude in the morning. Identifying people, experiences and achievements that give me a powerful sense of love, joy, happiness, and healthy pride. Family, health, business success, recognitions, projects coming full circle, being in nature, this is where I revisit those celebrations and am truly grateful.

The next song is a song for our darkness. Most people focus on their good things only, but polarities are to be properly managed and this includes our darkness and our light. This is where I release and surrender every thought of fear, doubt, shame, guilt, embarrassment, anger, frustration, rage, resentment, scarcity, and stress. I ask the Source to dissolve these emotions into its divine right plan for me, my family, and my organizations. Then I consume myself physically with the idea of letting these thoughts and emotions dominate me by holding my breath, tensing my body, and releasing it at the end of the song. I recognize my dark emotions and "burn" them, rather than letting them consume me during the day.

The next song is one involving power statements. I unleash at the top of my lungs with adamant physical gestures, chest pounding, swaying my arms, the statements that empower me to face the day and are representative of my abilities on this Earth. Some examples of my power statements are:

I'm a money and deal magnet! Only the very best deals flow to me and my organizations every single day!

I'm magician at turning assets into cash every day!

I'm a creative, smart, successful, complete finisher!

My organizations and I bring more value to the marketplace than anyone else!

I'm overwhelming value to all that I touch, creating impact and infinite abundance for my purpose!

Every day I build my legacy with clarity and intention and it is indestructible!

The last song is one of vision. Here I envision the details of my upcoming day and the results I want to have for that day. The second half of the song is dedicated to a three to five year vision for myself:

who I'm becoming, the abilities I need to develop to become that person, and the reality of my life in the future. If the time permits, I bookend with more meditation and quiet time.

As these set of songs finish and I move into my stretching, Chi-Kung, and at least fifteen minutes of intense exercise for the day. Once finished, I'm completely programmed like a primed assassin to overcome any obstacle, not only with force, focus, and precision, but also with a peaceful calm. This empowering alignment allows us to be hyper-aware of when we come into misalignment if we get frustrated, lash out at someone, or feel down. We can tap into our power plant of aligned energy and reset during the day, so we can continue to serve the marketplace and those we love.

A profitable restaurant is one that rotates the most tables. That means that we're consistently resetting the table, serving, and resetting the table again. Without embracing your own personal resetting ritual, you can never be prepared to serve others because it's inevitable that when you serve, things will get out of place, misaligned, and dirty. You need to reestablish your intentions, consistently and sustainably welcoming your sense of service in the process. You build a conscious awareness that you will have people in your "restaurant" and by resetting the table and laying out your "wares," you're open for business. Reset, serve, and repeat!

ALIGNING PASSIONS AND PURPOSE

Once you consistently execute your new morning resetting ritual, you can begin the work of understanding the difference between your life's purpose and your passion using your new awareness. By developing an understanding of purpose and passion, we can keep ourselves on the right path to building our strongest legacy with the greatest certainty in ourselves. Some people are lucky enough to identify their overlying passion very early on in life, and then there are those of us who have dozens of passions. Part of being aware of the legacy you're building is that you've had enough iterations to identify and refine your passions.

As you get older, your passions are more flexible. I don't know if it's my makeup as a serial entrepreneur, but I find passions in all my businesses. I'm sure that I would find passions in hundreds of other businesses. Passions are more particular, and opportunity based. Whereas there's a lot more commonality in our purpose as a species than there is in our passions. Purpose is the largest common denominator between humanity with the underlying emotion of love and service. Such as, someone's overall purpose might be to save nature or to save the planet. But their passion is saving cute, fluffy animals.

My purpose is to help people be more aware in their lives and how they can discover their greatness while pursuing their desired legacy. The key is to make sure your passion and purpose are interrelated, but that your passions don't detract from your purpose. By aligning yourself with your greatest purpose as well as forming an understanding of your passions and how those can deviate or align with your chosen purpose, you can weed out what doesn't serve your legacy. Then you're able to make intentional choices about what drives you forward and from where you can derive the most leverage. Our path to pursuing our purpose is one driven by our choice and free will. We are not forced to do so. By being so we are aligning ourselves for greatness.

3. BE THE CO-CREATOR OF YOUR OWN DESTINY.

At the end of the day, we must always carry with us the knowledge that we're the co-creators of our own destinies. By being intentional with our time and recognizing the importance of the little moments in life, modern men won't be so bogged down by the items on their to-do lists. The power of intention bleeds over into every area of our lives.

Once you recognize the power of ego, have an honest understanding of your mental, emotional, and spiritual energies, and can define your true purpose, you can acknowledge how to be the best co-creator of your legacy with Source.

The absolute example of a legacy champion is when we're in flow, in the zone, and everything is aligned so there's really no effort. It's flowing through us. We're like a portal into this other world of awesomeness and divinity. So we can be in flow, but it'll be hard for us to be grateful for that moment when we're in flow. We don't have an absolute awareness of flow while we're experiencing it, only that it feels amazing.

When we're out of flow, we'll say, "Wow, that was great." and we appreciate it. We need to tie together more celebration, recognition, and gratitude, because that's the momentum of our happiness. For me, it's an intentional purpose to, in the morning and at night, shower myself with gratitude, because that brings me energy, aligns my energy into that zone, an ability of expanded capacity and results. Once we step into gratitude and embrace our present situation as a worthy, special time, that's when we're able to reach past our basic selfish needs fed by ego to shift our energy in order to recognize those of importance around us.

CHALLENGES TO THE READER

1. If you're not physically active every day as a habit, integrate it into your lifestyle. Routines as little as fifteen minutes a day are effective if they are consistent! Define a reachable

one hundred-day goal and make a public declaration to family, at work or on a Facebook live. The more it scares you to declare it, the better. You'll be more likely to hold yourself accountable to your declaration.

2. If you're passionate about a sport or activity and have abandoned it due to a new or different lifestyle, give yourself the permission to begin it again. We come up with too many reasons why we can't do something. Find a way, create the environment, or find the closest replica to take its place. Align your dormant passions with purpose of creating more energy.

3. Find a physical challenge that scares you. Find a group to accomplish that task with them. Define a purpose for your commitment to succeeding with your goal. List at least five purposes and the emotions that stir in you from accomplishing this goal. You will need to have these clear when your mind tells you to quit and that it's not worth it. Study, train, rest, focus, and repeat until you accomplish your feat! Congratulations!

4. What is your biggest weakness when it comes to nutrition and health? Smoking, drinking, fast food, soda, desserts, frappuccinos? Whatever it is, dissect your pattern with it. When, where and why do you consume it? I challenge you to thirty days of sobriety from your biggest weakness. Find something healthy to take its place in your pattern. Make sure you have zero of this kryptonite in your home or office when you start this challenge. Make your challenge public and ask for help from those that surround you!

HOW THE ELEMENTS OF LEGACY INTEGRATE INTO ENERGY

LOVE

To have abundant and healthy physical, mental, emotional, and spiritual energy, we need love to be the driver of our power plant. If we're not aware that caring for ourselves is top priority, then our capacity to produce quality energy in these areas will be reduced. Having been over thirty pounds overweight and sluggish with low stamina levels while smoking, I definitely didn't love myself. My spirit was always a competitive athlete and one who loved being in motion. **It wasn't until I got fed up with my situation and decided to love and honor my true spirit, that I returned to producing sound and aligned high capacity energy to focus on all areas of my life and legacy.**

GROUNDED

The day has twenty-four hours, and as we get older we need to be sound stewards of the energy we devote to those hours. Although I can go a week straight sleeping limited hours a night, I know I'll be hitting a wall at a certain point. **The more we understand and listen to our bodies, the better we will take care of our energy production.** So, for all intents and purposes, we have finite energy levels, or at least peak levels. We can keep operating, but most likely at lower levels of yield. For example, I can find myself with enough energy to stay awake and be active, but to dedicate focused mental energy for thinking requires other conditions. Sometimes we're too tired to even fall asleep. Learning about our bodies requires interest, awareness, and iterations of driving ourselves to the limits so we can learn from them. Learn how to expand your finite levels of energy and do this realistically over a set period of time.

ABUNDANCE

To be productive, present, and expand your Legacy at the pace most of us would like to with the time we have left, well, let's just say we better get busy. As I told one of my managers the other day, I'd rather work with someone with high levels of energy and disposition than proven skills anytime. Why? **Because defense wins championships, and defense is played with energy and disposition.** Hustle. To achieve a consistent Legacy Lifestyle, we need to have abundant energy to be able to hustle and win. Win in every element of Legacy in order to achieve the goals and dreams we strive for in the long term. Alignment takes effort, focus, and doing the things most people are not willing to do. Consistently.

CONNECTION

Your energy can be scientifically explained. However, your entire existence is a feat only a higher consciousness or power could create. All of your involuntary bodily functions that work seamlessly to keep you alive and to heal are, in my opinion, one of God's greatest productions. To honor and understand that this ever-changing body temple is our only vessel while we're here, means **our bodies have been** divinely designed to adapt, change, and execute under all the conditions we put it through over time.

YOU

Let's understand energy as not only what allows us to be awake, active, and productive, but also that energy is completely unique to each of us. **It's our original and infinite signature we have in this world.** When your child feels safe with you, it's not because of your words or touch, it's your energy. When you walk into a room and people look up at you and feel something, it's because of your energy. The words you're reading now haven't kept you reading, but rather the energy behind this message. When people remember your name, they remember the energy of how you made them feel. We're energetic beings and the more we refine our unique energy signature, the more impactful our Legacy.

CHAPTER THREE
LEGACY ELEMENT
OF GROUNDED REALITY

As leaders who take risks, pressure is
inevitable. However, being drowned
by the pressure is optional.

Rocks

Rocks are the weight of the world
Every pain shame and human game
Is a heavy rock.
Everyone I see is holding huge rocks
Unable to move, feel, think, and be free.
Do not pass your rocks onto others
Especially your children.
Rock carrying is not my business
Rock throwing is.

- Gian Marco Palazio

I t was October 9th, 1999, my company was still a baby, I was twenty-three and leaving for Madison, Wisconsin, where the plan was for me to sell 50 percent of my company to an experienced gentleman who had become a distant mentor to me. He had fallen in love with Nicaragua and we hit it off. He was going to grow in new export markets, and I was going to count on his years of experience and millions of dollars of inventory to grow as well.

Early that morning, my father was still a month into recuperating from his quadruple open-heart surgery, and the doctor was at the house taking his blood for his normal six o'clock in the morning house call. I gave him a big hug and told him to be strong, although my voice probably quivered with nervousness because of the trip I was about to embark on that day. He held my hand, looked me in the eye, and told me in his debilitated, heavy English accent:

"Junior, you do good. Do good, Junior."

"I will, Dad, I will. I love you."

That night, while on a layover in Miami, I realized those were the last words we were ever going to exchange on Earth. My sense of reality shifted into a reality that was much less grounded and much more unstable. As a result, I had to build up my mental resources to keep myself emotionally together in an unstable time. This innate sense of resiliency is a tool we must build for ourselves and hone step by step in a process of staying grounded within our reality.

Our humanity is most resilient in desperate times and during deep challenges. We can mentally hunker down and convince ourselves to trudge through the worst of times. At the same time, our lives are so fragile. We don't know which day will be our last. Sometimes we're so sad but especially shocked by the news that someone is no longer here, which leaves us feeling vulnerable. That's a crucial time to rely on our sense of grounded reality and to feed into our excess energy that can get us through the tough, seemingly insurmountable times. Some tools that we can utilize during times of hardship where we need to endure include:

- Clarity of our current realities and situations.

- Embrace forgiveness of ourselves for our hardships.

- Devote ourselves to cultivating heightened awareness of our situation.

- Embrace abundant energy rather than dwelling in the negative. Give rather than expect.

A prime example of giving myself up to my reality and surrendering with a sense of self-forgiveness was when I had to crawl my way out of a financial snowball that was threatening to swallow my family and my legacy. Rather than giving into the negativity, which would have been the easier choice, I grounded myself using clarity, self-forgiveness, cultivating my heightened awareness, and embracing the true abundance of my reality without falling prey to feeding the flames of pessimism. I refused to get sucked into acknowledging that my life wouldn't get any better. Instead, I used the outlined steps to clarify a way out without lying to myself about my problems. This both paved the way for more abundance and increased my sense of pride so that I could tackle heavy issues, while remaining grounded in what I ultimately expected from my future as well as my legacy as a legacy champion.

My main business was not doing well. After years of important growth, we hadn't developed the precision to properly manage the real drivers of the business. I had committed the last significant portion of my family's nest egg to save the business. $2 million was to be executed over a period of six months to keep the business alive and stave off having to make the decision to close the doors. I was executing choices left and right to fight the inevitable and salvage my reality, but I wasn't addressing the real emotional tools needed to guide me out of my troubles.

During that year, I learned a few things: our cash flow wasn't going to turn around in time; our sales didn't grow at the rate we needed; and when I finally found the right industry coach for my business, to grasp the level of precision we needed to make the business work, it was quite possibly too little, too late. These lessons were super important, but I was more focused on the challenge of looking at my wife and telling her that our nest egg had been spent on more "lessons." As a provider and entrepreneur, this not only killed my sense of worthiness, but I started questioning my own abilities. That negativity and lack of self-worth only fed into my problems, which created more problems. I was ignoring my resiliency by refusing to be grounded. Instead, I was staying in my fear. Rather than harnessing my mental energies to go through the steps needed to turn my situation around in my brain, I gave in to my inner turmoil.

A year after committing our cash to the business, I was faced with the reality of closing a big part of our company. After making the eleventh hour full court presses to sell certain business units and not succeeding, I closed down two long-standing business units and let go of thirty-five great team members with hundreds of years of accumulated experience.

Needless to say, I didn't feel materially abundant. I felt like a failure, in the darkest time of my professional career and my life. As I mentioned in other chapters, my reality didn't start changing until I started to consciously surrender and release the weight of my expectations. I had to empty my negativity, accept my current reality, and practice self-forgiveness in order for my reality to shift into a more abundant place and make room for something positive to replace my perception.

Since I needed to assure my family's future and also create liquidity, I decided to put one of the first properties I ever purchased on the market. Someday this property was to become a small residential condominium, a project my wife was going to lead. We purchased it months before getting married. Now I was actively selling it and, surprisingly, I quickly had a few qualified buyers. As I efficiently started closing my business units and the cash flow from those operations improved as my fixed costs greatly reduced, I was able to pay off important company debts, and my mentality started morphing into a more positive sphere. I grew more confident and tried to get the best price for my property. As my energy became more abundant, I attracted better deals. By accepting my inner strength and my resiliency to restructure my financial legacy, I came to the table, which held my problems with better options, and was able to execute for my future to the best of my ability.

During the turmoil, I took my family on a meaningful summer vacation, all while my deal closed and the money was deposited into my account. I started relying on a more positive mind-set instead of wrapping chaos and fear around me like a blanket. Instead, by remaining grounded, I knew fully what I could take on in the future. Any threat to my legacy or my family didn't stand a chance with my refocused attitude. My sense of desperation fell away; we started gaining more business in the remaining units and our teams had more energy, so both my family, my business, and myself started reaping the positive benefits again.

As up and down as life is, I can honestly say that my material abundance is directly related to my feelings and my perception of my reality. If I decide I'm abundant, I will attract more abundance because I will become more attractive to others in my abundant reality. My teams will feed off that energy and likewise emit the same energy. This is such a powerful muscle to develop and a lesson I hope I don't have to relearn again in the future.

By remaining objective and following a set of concrete steps toward becoming grounded, I opened up my own perception of my reality to match my dreams and conquer my problems. Despite the negativity that the world throws at me, I'm secure in my ability to transcend past problems, navigate toward a sense of balance within my present, and execute with a sense of clear, focused urgency for my future. This allows me to remain grounded when teaching my children the same inner strength and abundant mind-set, while also knowing in my heart that any of my ancestor's choices that don't serve me today don't define my current reality.

GROUNDED IN OUR INFLUENCE WITH OUR CHILDREN

Your children and their impact on the world can sum up your legacy.

In the simplest of terms, your children and their impact on the world can sum up your legacy. However, we must take into account that everything we have in this life is rented and not permanent. This includes our children. We have the ability to persuade and mold them for about twenty-five years as their direct influencers. After that block of time, they'll consider us in their choices, but they'll largely make their own calls.

With that limited timeframe in mind, how do we bring up quality young men and women in a world full of entitlement, substance abuse, and constantly challenged values due to the media and outside influences? We must instill in them a sense of grounded reality while understanding that they're their own people, first and foremost, so we can provide the foundation for their resilient mind-set, but what they make of their life issues is in their hands alone.

They're not going to do what we tell them. It's the behaviors they see in us that they use as a model. We're their biggest influencers day-in and day-out. Children are sponges. They watch our actions, listen to our words, and feel the energy of our delivery when we speak to them. That is, until they decide we aren't such an influence due to our lack of relevance, presence, or love. Even though kids often don't have the maturity to understand our words, they have the ability since being in the womb to feel and perceive our emotional energies. With that in mind, the idea of building an intentional legacy becomes an urgent factor when we're younger parents, as opposed to when we're sixty. We have a better chance of imparting sound morals, wisdom, values, and legacy to our children when they're young, because we are conscious that we're being watched at all times. By grooming our children to define their own legacy without being beholden to life's natural troubles, we establish a sense of security for their future that will set them off on the right path to determine their own legacy.

The clock to leave our positive marks on our children starts counting early and if we're not conscious of the time limit, then we're the big losers. Urgency is key. We must understand the limits that are in place within our influential relationships with our children, so we can make the most intentional choices when it comes to raising them. Without understanding the consequences of our actions within a limited time frame, we can't begin to set a positive legacy example that they will look to later in life when it's time to define their own path.

For example, by being a role model for forgiveness with your children, you're teaching them as future legacy champions to not take themselves too seriously, and that humans are inherently flawed, so we will be hurt by others. My son has a friend that's on his sports team and he's a good kid. But he's gone through rough patches due to home issues and, as a result, he's not always that nice to the other kids including my son. My son is always supportive of him and wants to be his friend.

One afternoon after school I sat down with him and I said, "You know, your buddy is going through difficult times and he doesn't have the support system that you have at home. His dad probably doesn't talk to him like I talk to you, so he probably doesn't have that awareness. I think him being mean is his way of expressing himself and being frustrated, which is natural."

This conversation allows my son to have a better awareness to not take himself so seriously, not take others so seriously, understand that he's going to be hurt, and understand he's going to hurt others, whether it's intentional or not.

We've talked about him emotionally hurting other children's feelings, too. One day my son played an innocent joke on another kid who has some social challenges. The kid came up to him later and said, "Do you know what being empathetic means? I really don't appreciate that." And my son said, "Well, all I did was psyche you out." He didn't quite see the harm behind his joke.

To illustrate my point, I went through the process of putting my son in the kid's shoes while we stood in the busy public hallway of his school. After my demonstration, he became aware of the different circumstances that people might be going through that he isn't always aware of that could contribute to their feelings and point of view. By demonstrating to my son steps to remain grounded including embracing empathy, forgiveness, and an understanding of another's current reality, I was able to help him make smarter, more definitive choices with his classmates in the future.

Forgiveness is a key that opens many doors in life and those doorways lead to love. Forgiveness is a way of loving more. I talk to my kids about that all the time, because between themselves they have their own spats. As siblings, they need to consistently be forgiving themselves, moving on, and not holding grudges. This systematic process creates more grounded children, which sets them up through their lives to hone their inner strengths, make different choices than their ancestors, and own their own self-worth without falsely valuing themselves above others.

It's important when raising our children that they grow up understanding that they're loved, and that they are enough. Outside of these two factors, our children need different directions in terms of gender to get them off to a good start in life. For instance, with my sons I often contemplate when to expose them to the outside world, how to guide them in controlling their inner beasts/temper, teach them to treat and respect all the women in their lives as well as the women that are in their future, and how I can strive to be a strong example of guidance as well as discipline for them to model later in life.

For daughters, they require the same love on a day-to-day basis, but they require more present time with their fathers where they're offered one-on-one emotional support, safety, and security. They need an example that can be set by their fathers for their future partners in life. As well as what to expect in regards to the opposite sex in terms of respect, physical touch, and sex. There's also the delicate balance of understanding feminine energy and creating space for our daughters within that energy so they can flourish.

All our children must be raised with the understanding that we're not here to solve their problems for them, but we're able to offer a sounding board and solid, safe space for advice. We can guide them, but that shouldn't take away from the strength of their own choices. Only then can they become their own people. In order to parent in such a way to make that process possible, parents must keep up an open dialogue and parent by questioning their children's actions, their world, and their viewpoints. Through a growing awareness of our children's actions and reactions, as well as their triggers, they'll become more in tune with themselves at a young age, which sets the stage for their initiation into becoming a legacy champion.

Part of their new-found awareness that we bring into their lives as parents is their awareness of their ancestors, their lineage, and those people's prior legacy. Through an understanding of past traumas, the integral path of forgiveness, and an acceptance of their ancestors, children will be taught to forgive and become stronger as they build awareness for our mistakes, as well as their own possible choices when they become parents.

GROUNDED IN THE REALITY OF YOUR INHERITED LEGACY

What legacy does one inherit and what does one learn from their ancestors? You're aware that you've inherited their legacy, what that cost them, and what they went through to achieve their legacy. You learn what to do, what they did well that provided success, or how they established values and traditions that you value today. These stories then go on to inform your choices while expanding and ruling your own legacy. By being intentionally aware of their choices, we can either adjust or make the same mistakes.

What do we need to unlearn from our ancestors? What didn't work for them, so that we don't make their same mistakes and have to learn their lessons all over again? What examples did we see from our parents when they were under conflict or stress? Those are our current references with how we deal with those situations. We're constantly mirroring and being mirrored, even though we're not aware. Forgiveness is a process of weighing and contemplating these questions. It's coming to terms with the realities of our ancestors. It's releasing that weight.

UNLEARNING OUR ANCESTORS' MISTAKES

1. When were our parents under conflict or stress and how did that lead them to make choices for their legacy?

2. How do we mirror those choices in our own lives and how can we build up our awareness to break these patterns?

3. Can we take a step backward and survey their choices in the guise of forgiveness so that we can release the negative weight of their mistakes?

By answering these questions, we can get to a crux of our ancestral issues to transcend our past and move forward with a renewed sense of urgency to form our future legacy of our own choosing.

Often, we use our legacies as an excuse to shy away from reaching our highest potential or building onto our capacities as legacy champions. We say, "My dad did this," or, "He did that and that affected me." That's an excuse to stay stuck. But as we forgive our families for those mistakes, those burdens we're carrying as excuses, we release that weight we're carrying on our shoulders and in our hearts. We liberate ourselves from those excuses.

Forgiveness allows us to increase our capacity because we aren't limited by our judgment of our ancestors. It's easy for us to judge and say, "Oh my God, I can't believe he did that," or, "He was so weak in that area of his life that he wasn't able to put that in order." But to truly understand them is to put that judgement aside and become aware that we, as people, are imperfect. By being able to sympathize with their choices instead of using their mistakes as excuses to hold us back, we set ourselves free of our boundaries. We understand them, we love them, and we're empathetic to their process.

Then, if there are negative aspects of their legacy that we inherit, we have the ability to break what Eckhart Tolle calls "generational pain body." We can break their generational cycle and create a new one. Awareness, whether of the positive or negative, leads to the creation of a new understanding and a new cycle.

HOW TO BREAK THE ANCESTRAL CYCLE

1. Awareness of the impact of our ancestral choices.

2. A lack of judgement of them for those choices.

3. Understanding and empathy for their choices.

4. The gratitude they did the best with what they had at the time.

No matter what happens, what your country's been doing for the last fifty years, what the world's been doing, what your family's been doing—you have the ability to start anew and create whatever you desire. That's our ability, as human beings, as co-creators, to create a new cycle and a new legacy. This is a new opportunity and, eventually, a responsibility that we have for ourselves and for our future generations as legacy champions.

We're all a product of our ancestors' awareness and the best decisions available to them. This includes our genetics, family upbringing, and inherited wealth, in all senses of the word, as well as that of our communities. We inherit their religions, prejudices, and paradigms. Additionally, we inherit the history of our cities, countries, and the world in which we live every day. If you're from a small town in rural America with peace and friendliness instilled in its culture, but you move to a large cosmopolitan city, you will search to find pockets of that culture because it may remind you of the coziness of home.

While you may love being out of a small town because the trajectory of its culture is slow and relatively poor, you can use that experience and community legacy as something you choose not to actively follow in the future. Whether you choose to continue the legacy you inherited, that legacy has impacted, shaped and influenced who you are today.

It's important for our mental sanity to limit judgment of others, especially our ancestors, grandparents and parents. We may be highly critical of them and be at odds with why they made their choices. However, they made the best possible decisions with the options, awareness, and resources they had in that moment. I believe all people make their decisions with the best intent, even if they are destructive decisions. But those choices shouldn't define our legacy, rather they should inform our choices moving forward with an awareness that we can—and will—do better.

Most of our traumas are caused in a great majority by our parents. Whether we like it or not, our parents and their influence on our lives is what most defines and shapes our childhood. This is the influence of our subconscious, while we're in the process of maturing into beings that make aligned decisions in mind, body, and spirit. A child will make decisions independently of satisfying either one: mind, body, or spirit; but rarely all three aligned as a conscious decision. Unfortunately, most adults never add the spiritual part into their decision-making process until they are faced with challenges that are extremely painful.

While in India, during a week-long meditation retreat, I had an important breakthrough that pierced my consciousness. It came after a meditation where I traced myself back to my ancestors. What I did for the first time ever was be completely empathetic with each of my parents and their upbringing. I began to consciously understand their traumas (with my limited knowledge of their experiences) and understood how those manifested in their adult lives.

Each made their best effort to multiply their legacies in the best possible manner with the awareness, resources, and productivity they were able to acquire during their lifetime. They each did their best with the best of intentions. Dumping my judgment of their actions and gaining gratitude for their mistakes was a huge breakthrough for me, and one of unity, love, and timeless endearment. Many times we look back and criticize our parents, but that judgment is too easy, immature, and discounts our limited knowledge of all the facts. The acceptance of our inherited legacy, free of judgment, is the first step in being able to lay claim to becoming a legacy champion.

However, this is a lifelong marathon, not a quick sprint. Understand the urgency of the legacy task put before you, but rely on the resources inside and outside yourself to follow the path with renewed energy, clarity, and remain grounded to the idea that only we can shape our realities and only if we take the time to follow the proper steps.

Legacy is built on countless years of conscious, intentional practice, discipline, and awareness of why you do what you do. It's based on lifelong learning, respect, and gratitude for those that came before you and those that slay the dragons next to you. It's based on the constant connection to our Source for creativity, spiritual peace, and intangible fulfillment that money could never buy us. It's about becoming the creator of experiences born from the deepest recesses of your heart for yourself and your loved ones. It's our daily alignment of heart, mind, body, and soul by becoming a master of your own domain. Finally, it's a daily gratitude for having the opportunity to walk this Earth with timeless traditions and universal values, which can influence our fellow souls who desire to be exposed to those values.

It's based on being in touch with the most timeless emotion that has ever moved the world: love. With that sense of love comes the attitude that life's tough challenges will not seek to define us if we fully grasp our sense of abundance. If we continue to walk the path of our ancestors while being grounded in our reality, we can open the doors for bigger, better, and brighter choices in our lives because we've pushed off the negative mind-set that used to define us. We've begun the process to make room in our lives to be a true legacy champion because we carry the innate belief that we are worthy of it.

CHALLENGES TO THE READER

At what capacity and alignment are you currently operating in each of the following areas? Rate yourself from one to ten (ten being the highest).

_____ Intimate relationship

_____ Relationship with children

_____ Relationship with family

_____ Physical energy levels

_____ Body shape and fitness

_____ Overall health

_____ Business success

_____ Financial freedom

_____ Frequency of connection to your source

_____ Depth of connection to your source

_____ Living your passions

_____ Being certain of your purpose and living it enthusiastically

For your lowest three scores, make a one hundred-day plan to attend to those low areas every day and improve your score. Repeat this exercise every one hundred days and you will triple your overall capacity in one year. Make sure your short-term goals are aligned with your long-term vision for each category.

HOW THE ELEMENTS OF LEGACY INTEGRATE INTO GROUNDED REALITY

LOVE

I love to think of the future and all the possibilities for projects and experiences. However, I've come to really love my current reality. The now. **Where am I now compared to where I want to go in the future is my immediate feedback barometer.** Whenever I get excited about going forward toward a goal, I remember to revise where I am now in order to have clarity, as well as giving myself internal permission and freedom to act on my future dreams.

ENERGY

Our reality is our feedback machine, so if we apply all of our focused energy into remaining grounded in the here and now, we will move forward in our capacity because we won't be juggling so much of the everyday mental white noise and stress. That comes from dedicating our energy toward the future without being grateful and understanding of where we are in the world right this second. If we're out of shape, then we need to dedicate a lot of energy to this reality to get us in better shape. Intellectually, if our business is not reaching the numbers to be sustainable, then we need more energy to focus on the precision of our business and the same with our relationships and so forth in life. **Focus energies on your current realities to create the change you desire in your Legacy, only then will your energy come from a grounded and whole place.**

ABUNDANCE

Someone who's abundant in their grounded reality is extremely disciplined. Most people measure the heck out of their businesses and have those indicators or numbers down pat, but you'd be surprised how many entrepreneurs don't take those extra steps to be diligent.

I've become fascinated by the measurement of nearly all aspects of my life, not only business elements, but personal indicators. There's a discipline to logging your exercise rep count, meditation, relationship habits, every cent of income and every cent of expenses, bad habits and yes, even intimacy with your spouse. I measure it all. **By focusing my energy in a disciplined manner, it gives me a constant reminder of where I am in my legacy journey and allows my autopilot of Legacy correction to function with ease.** Are you willing to do what most people aren't willing to do? It will take abundance in your grounded reality.

CONNECTION

As my connection to my Source expands I've come to understand that we're timeless beings. Although that concept may be hard to comprehend, **by being connected in my current grounded reality I clearly understand that any future I desire is already a reality.** My past, present, and future are one in the same. The best example of this concept is nature. When I go to the top of a volcano and indulge in that magical view, I'm only experiencing that because I'm present in the moment. But the volcano, the view, is always there, as it was yesterday as it will be tomorrow. It's timeless. That's why I have so much appreciation for my connection to my current reality.

YOU

When our Legacy is expanding we're transcending because our frequency is operating at a higher capacity like RPM's in a sports car. **The more you operate at a higher frequency, the more you need to shift to a higher gear.** There is always another level. Knowing that this is your unique process, you might as well love it as a process of Legacy expansion and not a destination of Legacy perfection.

CHAPTER FOUR
LEGACY ELEMENT OF ABUNDANCE

Work diligently with the lightness and creativity of a spontaneous, curious child.

My last summer internship in college was with the international franchise department of a global fast food chain conglomerate with multiple brands. I had a great experience and found my first corporate mentor. The job opened up my worldview, while putting me in uncomfortable positions that helped me expand as a person and as an eventual entrepreneur. This was one of those opportunities that opened my mind-set up to the abundance that was all around me. After that experience, I always thought, like many entrepreneurial efforts, that I'd have a food business. I had a feeling that someday this initial experience would come back to me and I would venture into the industry once again, this time as an entrepreneur.

As a kid, I grew up going to a chicken rotisserie shop, which turned out to be the original location of a great rotisserie chicken chain. Fifteen years later, when the opportunity appeared for me to be a part of the chain in the tourism capital of my country, I didn't even blink. It was a dream come true. The right brand, the right location, and an investment I wanted to add to my portfolio.

After two years of hard work, a grand opening to huge fanfare, and three partners, I was closing the place down with nearly all the shares in my name. I learned many lessons during that experience of loss which contributed to my abundance awareness including:

- be wary of getting into a deal late in its conception;

- never be the only partner with cash, unless you plan to be the only partner;

- pick partners based on business philosophy, not convenience;

- a partner must bring strategic value, not just sweat equity;

- have a flexible landlord; and

- make sure the franchisor is willing to save his brand in your market.

What I got from my stint with the franchise was great operational experience, a lifelong friendship with one of my partners as well as another project together, and a basis for the success of our current coffee chain. These experiences helped form me to be able to attract the best possible team and additional experience in the food industry to put together a winning concept that we have been working on the last eight years. Abundance feeds into abundance. Likewise, failure can lead to abundance. Each mental shift toward the idea that my life was abundant brought me closer to what I truly wanted as a legacy champion. Good experiences and what we take away from the failures propel us into further positive experiences, which seal our fate as the creators of our legacies. Today, one of our units is in that same tourism capital as the franchise I had to shut down and has a great position with a solid landlord and does very well.

This chain of experiences has challenged me but has also formed a better understanding for me of what it means to create value and abundance for others. This value creation is our business legacy, if we're able to consistently keep adding value. When you think your experiences are discounting you and causing economic loss, do what needs to be done. But remember to trust in the process. If we remain certain that all of our challenging experiences are there to add value to our business sense as entrepreneurs and as people, we can learn to spot eventual growth in our businesses within these struggles and lean on an abundance mind-set to get us onto less shaky ground. Then those experiences that are challenging will be more than valuable as well as abundant in the knowledge we've gained from them.

THE IMPACT OF HAVING AN ABUNDANT MIND-SET

1. Abundance breeds more abundance.

2. By cultivating an abundance mind-set, you bring abundance to everyone around you.

3. We can learn to spot abundance in the worst situations which allows us to plan for possible detours on our road to becoming a legacy champion.

Today my chain of stores is at least fifteen times the value of the economic loss I had in my previous venture when I first started out. When you lead with abundance, abundance follows suit. We only need to remember to cultivate and build up our skillset in recognizing abundance to activate it to our full potential. Be an abundant leader to your people, teach them what you know, and allow them to flourish with you. Be abundant with your energy and enthusiasm towards the marketplace and create experiences that others value. Be abundant with those you learn from with your gratitude and be abundant to those who follow, as being a mentor to others serves the entire community. Once we've maximized our awareness, understanding that abundance is all around us, we can channel that abundance into every facet of our lives, including building our legacy within the business marketplace.

Steps to Build an Abundant Legacy Marketplace

1. Build the right business relationships.

2. Find and create your tribe.

3. Influence your teams.

4. Trust versus control in business.

5. Acknowledge achievement.

Here are five key components to bringing value and abundance to the marketplace and creating a Legacy of Abundance:

1. BUILD THE RIGHT BUSINESS RELATIONSHIPS

Business relationships play a large role in a successful and abundant legacy. I look at business relationships as a long-term issue that we must actively cultivate. Long-term business relationships are based on trust and the actions that support one's word, which are the defining aspects of a great reputation. Today's business world is based on brand value, whether that is someone's personal brand or a company brand.

Legacy in business is your brand. This brand takes a long time to build and very little time to break the trust that upholds your business in the eyes of the marketplace.

Legacy in business is your brand.

When you're true to your values in business, and thus your brand, you will be very transparent to others in your business relationships. It's very easy to count on someone that has solid values because you know you can count on them explicitly, due to their honesty and upfront communication. It's the same with any brand. People I've seen in business that have flexible morals or flexible values usually have a weak legacy. Most often they're not solid in their business foundation, which can lead to making promises they're unable to keep because they're not solid in their brand values and are eager to do business regardless of anything that might be damaging.

For instance, you can either have the short-term convenience of a business partnership which has flexible values but checks all the boxes in the rushed time period you require, or you can carve out intentional business relationships. These business relationships have long-term value creation. Long-term positions bring bigger and better opportunities versus a quick fix for the business's consistency to their value system and their transparency with your company.

Your leadership is being observed and the impact of your influence is important because it flows forward into the world as an act of abundance, which keeps the positivity flowing toward your business. Your business is the biggest leverage tool you can have regarding your overall abundance impact. Within your relationships, there's an impact pyramid that rates those relationships based on their influence within your life and on their interaction with you on a day-to-day basis. This includes five levels:

FIVE LEVELS OF LEGACY IMPACT

1. Anyone who you interact with multiple times a week, on a deeper basis including extended conversations. Those influenced include immediate family, direct reports, best friends, coaches, partners, peers and colleagues, and clients with a high interaction level.

2. Anyone who interacts with you two to five times a month. Those influenced include extended family, friends, mentors or mentees, and middle managers or colleagues in other locations.

3. Anyone who you interact with once a month. Though there's limited personal interaction, these people know who you are, what you do, and how you do it.

4. Social media followers on all your channels.

5. Active clients attended by your businesses in the last year. Considering each unique client as an individual or company who did business with your company in the last year.

If you wish to measure your Legacy Impact Indicator, please visit my website at: **www.gmpalazio.com/legacyimpact**.

As entrepreneurs, being lonely at the top, we have to find support systems or people who help us in order to further our abundance, as well as grow our abundance impact outside our small circle into the world. We must ask for help to grow abundant. My father used to tell us, "Don't ask for any favors so you don't owe anyone anything." It was a generational and idiosyncratic cultural issue where he grew up and learned to do business. Mostly because politics were intermingled with the business environment. But this can be close-minded in our society today, where an abundance mind-set embraces helping others as a way to reap more positive rewards outside of typical selfish networking skills.

We live in a much more collaborative and networked world today and because of that, as I began growing professionally, I lost the belief that asking for help was weak. I became adept at asking for help, seeing it as a necessary element for growth and upward mobility. Not as a selfish favor, but because I was the first one to offer my help to others in need. If you consistently ask for help and don't offer yourself or give back to people that could use a mentor or support, then you're acquiring favors. But if you're the first one to offer yourself, then I see it as the regular interchange of healthy energy.

When I started my formal entrepreneurial activities, there was a generation of businesspeople that knew it all. You couldn't tell them anything. They weren't willing to learn anything. That was shocking to me and went against everything I felt about business and life. So I applied this saying, "Know-it-alls will never know." Becoming a student of life, business, and humbly, of others, is key to growing and leading teams. We have to be heavily focused on strategies that attract, recruit, and create people-centric, positive cultures in the workplace. In order to build a business and be able to handle multiple operations at once, you must build teams that are drawn together by values, a common mission and a way of doing things. Only then can you cultivate abundance within your teams, because they are carrying the openness within themselves to be receptive to new knowledge and build on each other, which opens new doorways to being abundant.

2. FIND AND CREATE YOUR TRIBE

Without attracting the best people, you will never grow. We all want control; we all want certainty. Most humans have certainty as one of their top two of the six basic human needs[4] as noted by Tony Robbins, in his "6 Basic Needs That Make Us Tick."[5] Certainty strengthens our ego and overshadows our awareness of the impact of our actions on others. Additionally, it closes our mind to new solutions and the flexibility required in today's ever-changing business world. Leveraging others' time and material resources is a basic concept of the multiplication of abundance.

We need to wake up to the fact that we're not so damn important, and we definitely shouldn't take ourselves too seriously. You can only laugh at yourself in public if you aren't attached to your certainty and significance. Your ego would never allow it. So why are we the ones with all the right answers? Why do we have "yes people" in our organizations? Why don't we hire people smarter than ourselves? To grow, we must challenge these old habits and become humble servant leaders that have egos ready to go when called upon, because it's neither healthy nor smart to have no ego, but it should only be a reference point.

There are several ways to create a knowledgeable team that can help you reach your entrepreneurial goals:

- **Trust others:** The only way to keep your glass half-empty to receive new ideas is to empty that glass by trusting others are doing what they need to do. Most small-sized entrepreneurs struggle with this and believe that, due to their technical expertise or passion, they should be the center of operations for their business. Be comfortable with more delegation. Trust but verify.

---

4   The six basic human needs are: the needs of the ego, certainty, uncertainty, significance, love/connection, the needs of the soul, growth, and contribution.

5   Tony Robbins, "Tony Robbins: 6 Basic Needs That Make Us Tick," *Entrepreneur*, accessed May 31, 2018, https://www.entrepreneur.com/article/240441.

- **Be vulnerable:** An innovative leader must be surrounded by people who allow them to open up their vulnerabilities in all areas of their life. Since it's lonely at the top, it's important for the entrepreneur to find a mastermind, a forum, or a group where they're growing and to bring back their personal growth to the organization.

- **Find a tribe outside of your business:** Your organization is your canvas as an artist. But you must personally be refining yourself in another creative arena, with other people, before excelling on your canvas. We must have other areas of our lives where we're growing our capacity and refining ourselves. That way we come back to the organization as a more refined leader.

Most people think their company is where they're doing all their growth. Where they're doing their relationship growth, their material growth, and their personal challenges. But that's where you put what you learn in the outside world to work. Your business isn't necessarily the fountain of all your learning. You will learn from your business, but it can't be the only place. It's highly expensive and potentially disastrous that your business be your only space for trial, error, and honest feedback. True growth means opening ourselves up to honest feedback so we can recharge our sense of awareness within our situation and recalibrate our choices so we reap our best chances of reward.

3. INFLUENCE YOUR TEAMS

Anytime I have personally gone through a stressful experience with a group of people, whether it's a sports team, a class, a fraternity, a retreat, or a business team, there's an immediate, lifelong bond that's created because we've acted and united under pressure and confronted a challenge. This is one of the most powerful experiences that we have as a species, uniting under a common cause and working together under stress.

To be able to lead a team in a constant process as a leader is an honor and it's a huge responsibility. Teams should challenge each other, recognize each other, and ask more of each other, because your capacity increases as you win more victories and respond to more challenges together. As your team's capacity increases, your legacy also increases, as well as those of your team members. When our families, our clients, or our communities show this growth, it's clear we're living in our abundance mind-set. Three concepts that promote team and individual growth are:

- **Vulnerability:** Nothing builds trust more than vulnerability. As you expose your vulnerabilities and your desires to people, it's difficult for others not to be empathetic or even assist you in reaching your goal. This is the same as when we actively listen, and we're not shut down by "our way is the only way." Actively listening is a way of being vulnerable because it allows you to question your own beliefs. This is a great place for growth to occur.

- **Gratitude:** When I'm a witness to others who are going through a tough time, expose my own shortcomings and challenges, or when others listen and support me, I'm showered with gratitude. This puts life into perspective and it unites us under some of the biggest common denominators of humanity. We're more alike than different.

- **Inspiration:** When we're witness to others achieving their goals and being great at what they do, we're inspired to grow closer to achieving our own goals. It acts as a fuel for us to act more diligently and shed our limiting beliefs. While understanding that our processes, needs, and desires are unique but very similar.

4. TRUST VERSUS CONTROL IN BUSINESS

Trust sets up a more powerful platform than control, because it frees you up to follow your purpose and lead your teams, instead of bogging yourself down with trying to do everything for your business yourself. Many times, our job as entrepreneurs is to set the stage for our teams, clear the road of obstacles and develop them along the way. To guide others to unleash their gifts and their talents for the mission at hand. The more entrepreneurs understand themselves, the more success they'll have because they'll know how to better run their teams.

We have to understand what drives our employees crazy and their unique abilities. For example, it's mostly detail-oriented things for me, because that's one of my unique abilities. I'm going to come in and be heavily detail-oriented when it's a customer experience. I'll say, "All right. Put yourself in the customer's shoes. What is she going to see? Where is she going to sit? What's she going to ask for? What's going to be her cycle, her path of experience while she's here?"

But I'm not going to get in the way of my people unleashing their gifts, especially if they have talents that complement mine. So getting out of your organization's own way is a huge ability to develop as an entrepreneur who wants to build a solid legacy foundation for their business. Many times, we're the barrier that kept innovation and other peoples' gifts and talents from being realized to better our business.

Micro-management is the killer of so many businesses, but mostly that's because of the mentality of the entrepreneur. Everyone is here to teach you *something*. Especially those without the diplomas and the ones that drive you crazy. Why? Because they teach you how you react to situations where you don't have control. How you react to life when things aren't done your way. It feels so good to be right. But when we become married to having all the answers, then we stop listening to others and seeing other's points of view. Keith Cunningham says, "You try to be right so often you become dead right,"[6] because you're right, but dead in value to the market and nobody wants to work with you.

Trust and positive motivation can be much more effective tools than control in your business management style because it opens your mind to new ideas, flexibility, and helps you become a humble business leader that doesn't lead with your ego. The only way to grow a company with competent professionals and to create a culture that attracts likes and expels dislikes is to release the grip on control. The best business leaders have the best cultures, empower their people, and push a handful of large ideas throughout the organization. Lead by example, constantly question, and find innovative ways to deliver value, because as Tony Robbins says, "the biggest limit on any company is the psychology of the business owner."[7]

You can't create a legacy while juggling a non-functioning, non-cohesive team that relies on you as the boss to establish trust, specific roles, and boundaries. By surrounding yourself with the right people and nurturing the right culture, you create an environment that's ripe

---

6   Keith Cunninghamn, "Wealth Mastery," (live event, Savusavu, Fiji, March 2012).
7   Tony Robbins, "Business Mastery," (live event, Las Vegas, NV, January 2013).

for success. Which allows you to spend an equal amount of time on other areas that matter in life such as family, friends, self-care, and spiritual time. These small allotments of time build up into a solid factor for success, which sets the stage for abundance to roll into our lives and compound not only our time but our overall results.

5. ACKNOWLEDGE ACHIEVEMENT

Both achievement and ambition are healthy, when they're a peaceful byproduct of our overall legacy path. I've become focused on elevating my capacity by just one more notch every day. Our internal worth, free of ego, titles, and toys, is really what we need to find to be able to have complete certainty over the long-term in our lives. To build abundance in our lives, we must build our strength by counting and feeling gratitude for our happy moments.

You should acknowledge your moments of achievement, where you find success, connection, satisfaction, and fulfillment in your everyday life. As well as maximize that feeling that acknowledgement brings in order to grow to your highest potential. There are several ways to go through the process of understanding and maximizing our sense of accomplishment:

- **Celebrate victories:** Something I've learned is we need to celebrate our victories twice as much as we focus on our failures. Most people spend a large amount of time on their failures and they discount their victories. This is something I've been applying in my business during the last couple of years. If you're not in a great place, you need to start getting accustomed to winning again. By putting yourself in an achievement-focused headspace and counting your little victories, you can become more aligned with positivity.

That's an extremely important energy shift. Nothing attracts success like a winning attitude and success itself.

- **Gratitude:** I shower myself with gratitude twice a day. I do it in my morning ritual and in the evenings when I pray with my kids. We're grateful for everything from the roof over our heads, to the families that support our employees that support us, to Mother Nature. We go through these gratitude lists and we're aware of them and we're bringing them to the forefront of our consciousness and everyday experience.

- **Humility:** I write my lessons of humility every day in my journal. What I went through that day as well as what I extracted from it and the gratitude I have from my experiences. A daily acknowledgement knowing that I'm replaceable and that any day can be my last.

- **Less structure with our happiness:** We put too many rules on ourselves for our own happiness. These rules are rarely satisfied and very hard to achieve. The more we let go of our rules, conditioning, and requirements that we self-impose to be happy, the more we allow ourselves to find the daily joy in the small things in life.

Throughout our business lives, our legacy will be built within the values, emotions, and growth that we allow to flourish within our teams. By acknowledging our business team's unique gifts, our own limitations, and trusting that we've picked the right people to walk beside us to carry out our dreams to our highest potential within their own and our own capacity, we're leaving a strong, airtight legacy. An important part of the process is establishing our own internal growth outside of the business so that we can fold in those ideas and structures of new knowledge into our business. This outside canvas is important to develop instead of relying on our business to teach us everything, which puts too much pressure on a large portion of our legacy, while discounting our outside influences that determine our life changes outside of the office.

Part of being a legacy champion involves being honest within every aspect of our lives. This includes acknowledging and being grateful for the abundance of positive choices and circumstances within both our lives and business situations. We also must acknowledge how we relate to our business, successes, failures, teams, and missions, and whether we're balancing our other life areas within our legacy system. Without being aware of our intentions and business legacy, we can't grow our capacities or our abilities to accept positive changes into our lives. Likewise, we can't open ourselves up and make the right choices to build a strong future with confidence.

CHALLENGES FOR THE READER

1. What is the frequency and precision of your business abundance alignment?

    - How often do you meet with your management teams?
    - How structured are your meetings?
    - Are there alignment indicators visible to everyone in the meeting? Are you being told things you don't want to hear?

    Look to create the discipline of alignment with your teams through weekly and daily huddles in order to encourage communication, reinforce focus, and remove bottlenecks.

    - How often are you visiting your personal balance sheet?
    - Are you keeping a monthly business, family, and personal budget?
    - Are you saving money for options, opportunities, and desires?
    - Are you achieving your vacation days per year that you targeted?

    Maintain a disciplined frequency of your personal abundance measurements to make sure you're on the right track.

2. How detailed, precise, and investigative is your recruiting process? As an entrepreneur, how detailed is your interview process? This question takes into account working relationships because who you choose to associate with is one of the most important decisions in your life. How documented are you about bringing on new people? For more information on hiring as well as making sure you're implementing the correct process, I suggest the book *Who,* by Geoff Smart, or the bible of hiring processes,

Topgrading, by Bradford Smart. Both resources will give you the best recruiting systems and show you how to develop A-players within your teams.

3. Do you know your own unique abilities? Find your unique ability by interviewing at least five to seven of your closest colleagues, partners, and friends who know how you work because they're the most likely to be the most straightforward and honest. Don't include close family until the end when you have your results. Ask your pool of people these questions:

    1) What is the most significant impact that I have had on your life?

    2) When I'm at my best or you've seen me at my best, what do you observe/experience from me?

    3) How can I have the greatest positive impact on others/ the world?

    4) What is the one thing that I can do better in order to increase my impact on you and the world?

    5) Find the common themes in their answers and verify with your own feelings as well as with close family members.

This is the quick and easy way. Or you can reach out to Julia Waller at Strategic Coach and read her book, *Unique Ability 2.0 Discovery.*[8]

Once our unique abilities are clear and verified, begin delegating most other work to your team and focusing your energy and intent on these unique abilities. As a result, you will be more empowered and passionate with your daily work.

---

8   Catherine Nomura, Julia Waller, and Shannon Waller, *Unique Ability 2.0 Discovery: Define Your Best Self* (Toronto: Strategic Coach, 2015).

HOW THE ELEMENTS OF LEGACY INTEGRATE INTO ABUNDANCE

LOVE

This is probably the easiest element to understand and desire out of all the others. We all love abundance. Having excess money, time, knowledge, love, friends, experiences, and connection to Source makes us all feel awesome. It's easy to have an abundance mind-set when all this is present. But how can you love to be abundant when you're challenged or going through a cash crunch. Will you adjust and turn on that love of abundance? **Let me tell you that our alignment for the love of abundance starts within us and is accelerated by clarity.** When done correctly, it allows us to feel free of our mind's limitations we instill in ourselves. When I was most financially challenged, I worked hard to feel abundant, even though my reality was otherwise. It wasn't until I was in alignment with abundant energy that my situation began to change to a new, more abundant reality.

ENERGY

Abundance is energy, and a powerful one. It's one that has been written about excessively. I'll just remind you that when you align yourself with this energy you will reproduce abundance. You can't listen to the football game on the radio if you're in the frequency of a public radio station. You must align with that specific energy to listen, feel, and manifest abundance. **Focus your energy on the proper frequencies, even** though your environment isn't always in line with that feedback. Brainwash yourself? Not necessarily, just desire abundance, feel it, and know you're a creator of this energy.

GROUNDED

In Luke 20:45-21:4, we read about the poor widow who offered two simple copper coins to the temple treasury, while the rich wore expensive clothing, made long rambling speeches and gave a lot of money to impress others in their community. Jesus noticed how the poor widow had given more than anyone else because of what it meant to her. We must understand from that example that our abundance is proportional to our reality. When we compare ourselves to our neighbor, we're doing our Legacy a disservice. Your Legacy is unique, not to be compared, only to be tested and challenged by the highest version of yourself that you can imagine.

CONNECTION

Our Source is infinite in its abundant energy, and when we feel that connection with abundance, we know a special sense of peace. We were designed to be able to experience the riches of life and the lack of mind-set we have adapted from our learned limitations only gets in our way. The more we shed this learned limitation mentality, the freer we are to connect to our birthright of abundant energy and resources. There are more than enough physical resources in the world to go around for everyone to feel abundant. Your Source desires that for your own experience.

YOU

Nobody is going to come save you. **Your abundance mind-set is up to you to cultivate and tend to on a daily basis.** It's your responsibility and duty to create an abundant Legacy. As the popular saying goes, "You must participate in your own rescue!" As a leader and Legacy Champion, your abundance is necessary in all areas to properly rule and expand your Legacy.

CHAPTER FIVE

LEGACY ELEMENT OF CONNECTION TO SOURCE

There has never been a place so warm and cozy as my soul, and a place so dark and cold as my own mind.

In beautiful Udaipur, India, toward the end of my week-long meditation retreat, I was physically and emotionally exhausted. The days were long, and I'd never been exposed to such extended meditation sessions. The stillness and injection of consciousness that I was experiencing in the sessions was taxing my body until I was laughing, crying, and entirely giving in to my spirit. I was connecting to my Source in a way I never thought was possible before with a depth that connected me to all my past problems, wiped them away, and made a path for forgiveness, allowing me to serve for generations with the sense of urgency needed to appreciate the future project I'd taken on by becoming a legacy champion.

Another realization that came through to me during my meditation retreat is that time doesn't exist because it's a human construct. We're spiritual beings and live forever. Those aspects that we deem either negative or positive truly have no meaning outside of the human mind and, as a result, offer us learning opportunities. The negative experiences are, for the most part, experiences of pain. Positive experiences are usually experiences of pleasure. There are usually more learning opportunities taken from negative experiences than from positive ones, because of our habit of going back and seeing our mistakes.

By releasing my attachment to judgment and judging my experiences, I began to understand that all experiences are of equal value, whether negative or positive, whether major or minor. A big business deal is equal to an argument with your wife. We're attached to identifying our processes into categories of judgment based on our limited worldly measurements. But none of those judgements have to remain with us.

Our lack of judgement keeps us grounded because we understand everything in this life is rented—our businesses, homes, relationships, children, and bodies. In a timeless, cosmic sense, none of our Earthly world goes with us, only our experiences, and how we consciously elevate others and ourselves, depart as we do. That, in a nutshell, will be our legacy for the world that remains.

Your ancestors are an important precursor to shaping and influencing who you are as a person. As you accept without judgement or criticism, and sometimes forgive, their legacy's impact on you, you draw closer to embracing your own legacy and taking control of your future. By transcending the past, you gain unlimited sense of control, balance your present with a lack of judgement, and urgently usher in your future. You allow yourself to serve others with your legacy for generations.

Building a spiritual legacy starts by forging and encouraging a relationship or conversation with your Source. Source is God, the Divine, our creator, whatever we recognize as the governing force or energy that created the universe. It's also the universal intelligence behind Mother Nature, our involuntary body functions, and the massive amount of coincidences that appear in everyone's lives.

My personal inner conversation with my Source led me to write this book. I always knew I wanted to write a book. As my passions became clearer and my unique abilities became more apparent, I started a conscious conversation with Source through which I was told to write this book and share my experiences.

This project wasn't taken on with a "Wouldn't it be a great business idea to tell people about my experiences?" outlook, or with any grandiose ideas of great success or fame. It was told to me from an inner Voice of Source, so I listened and acted on what it told me. The funny part was that Source's instruction came to me when I doubted myself the most in my business, career, and life. When I felt most exposed and embarrassed by a temporary setback. When I took on this book project, it was done without external confidence but with full internal certainty, granted to me by having a constant relationship with my Source.

How to Build a Legacy Connection with Source

1. Shower in gratitude

2. Recognize your power of manifestation

3. Visualize as reality

4. Have faith in Source's guidance

5. Empty the cup and listen

Our spiritual legacy will manifest in an intangible arena of our internal peace, gratitude, and certainty. But will multiply itself in tangible areas of our legacy like love, energy, and abundance. Once we're working toward being in alignment with our Source or refining our spiritual energy, building emotional awareness and gratitude for what we have in the present moment, we'll build up our capacity to recognize life's daily magic on a moment-to-moment basis. All areas of our lives will improve over time as our relationship becomes deeper and stronger.

As our passions and daily challenges become more demanding, it only becomes more important to start increasing our spiritual capacity as well as to take time to connect with our gratitude. It's much easier to find ways to have more energy and mental aperture to withstand the demands and pressures we encounter as a regular giver in our world with a centered mind-set. You should acknowledge this sense of privilege because you're being asked to step up and take a role of leadership and responsibility. As your roles in life expand, so do your capacities, which in turn opens the way for new and bigger opportunities to create your legacy.

While expanding my Legacy, I have found five significant ways to develop a connection with your Legacy Source:

1. SHOWER IN GRATITUDE

You, as a human being, were made to be filled and blessed by being in alignment with Source energy. Alignment is a mentality that you can harness to change the energy of your life. By accepting and refining your ability to feel and see abundance, you open yourself up to positive change and good intentions. You're able to guide these changes by using your positive thoughts to bring positive outcomes into your life.

Gratitude comes easily for me.

I shower four times a day: once with cold water, once with warm water, and twice with gratitude. I bookend my days with gratitude by embracing joy, love, healthy pride, and during gratitude prayers with my children. When we're full of gratitude, there is space for nothing else and it's easy to create momentum for your past, present, and future desires.

> I shower four times a day: once with cold water, once with warm water, and twice with gratitude.

2. RECOGNIZE YOUR POWER OF MANIFESTATION

Trusting in your ability to manifest your physical realities means understanding that each of your thoughts has an energy flow that circles and twists around you. These thoughts are birthed by powerful emotions that stir you such as rage, hopelessness, excitement, and enthusiasm. This energy only attracts other energy that's the same in its intention. Therefore, if you think of a desire with powerful emotional anchors, the energy you bring into your life is aligned to that desire.

By banishing your negative thought patterns, you open yourself up to the universe serving you more pleasant, abundant life choices. These thoughts eventually transform into words, which then transform into actions, which finally become your desired reality. Manifesting our desires is one of the highest forms of spirituality in our world. In every business that I've started, manifestation has been a conscious process of awareness. That's why I consider business a spiritual process in and of itself.

Manifestation is like tuning into the right radio station, it has to be on the same frequency to come in clearly. Aligning our intentional energy is much the same way. One way to influence your desires is to envision your life exactly as you want it to unfold in the future and know with certainty that it will be a reality in your life. By keeping a constant, intentional sense of awareness throughout your day, month, or year, you ground and focus yourself to achieve your desired results.

3. VISUALIZE AS REALITY

I started visualizing my desires at a very young age, as most kids naturally do. I found myself daydreaming, sketching, acting out in my head or even playing out my desires for my life. These visualizations or playacting were usually based around girls, sports, or beating my rival friend at school in a race or a soccer game. They were filled with details, words, and emotions in the moment as if that visualization were true and a part of my reality. As I progressed into an adult, my visualizations became more about my future, getting into a university, how to solve tough school subjects, and eventually how to resolve my first business problems.

By trusting the powers of manifestation and visualization as tools to help you live your best, most well-intentioned life, you can embrace your faith in the process of change with the freedom to start anew and adjust your ongoing course for the future, which is key to manifestation. Faith in your sense of Source, in your ability to hope, and in your knowledge, that tomorrow is another day.

Most of my greatest moments within my business, family, or personal accomplishments I've imagined for years or many months before they became reality.

4. HAVE FAITH IN SOURCE'S GUIDANCE

There are so many events in my life that I say to myself, "there's no way that's a coincidence." Life, in general, has an uncanny way of just adding up. Through our filters and experiences, we all believe different things about our universe. I believe and trust God, the Source, guides us. This is not a passive guidance system, but a very active one. The problem is we're rarely in tune with our guidance system's active functioning. How can Waze help you if you never open the app? Well, this is much the same way. If your doubting your connection and faith to guide you, well then, your guidance app won't work because it's not even open.

The more we develop our connection abilities, the more constant our guidance system becomes within us. Sometimes it's easier to identify our Source guidance app working over the long-term rather than during the day-to-day. Mainly because we're more open to noticing long term results, for example, if I hadn't broken up with a girlfriend of many years, I would have never met my future wife. We wouldn't have created the fulfilling life and family we are blessed with today.

The fact that I had to close part of my distribution business in order to focus on writing this book and sharing my story's message is now clear to me. Many times, we're in a dark or difficult place when our Source guidance app kicks into high gear. Will we always understand why we're at a certain place in our lives? No. But trust the fact that we're being guided somewhere important and we must allow ourselves to be guided. We need to listen up. We're constantly being spoken to by our connection with the universe, just as our Source guidance app is constantly recalculating our quickest route to our manifested futures, so we can adjust our course, our mind-set, or surrender to another path. When we listen and accept Source guidance, we become lighter and we can act more efficiently to create our best future outcomes.

However, faith, on its own, is an insufficient source for changing our reality within our legacy plan. We also need to be in the zone and hustle to make our best lives possible for ourselves and those around us. We need to participate in our own rescue through focused action. When you're in the zone we feel selflessness, timelessness, effortlessness, and richness. This is referred to as the STER of altered states in *Stealing Fire* by Kotler and Wheal. When we're aligned with our best capabilities we're able to manipulate the present moment to reflect our best self. By truly being present, we acknowledge that our uniqueness and our place in the world is perfect where we are right now.

One of the ways to keep that awareness in the forefront of our mind is to use affirmations or power statements, which are phrases we can use to reinforce anchoring emotions in our consciousness. Power statements are expressed with heavy emotion and commanding voice which allows us to learn and help program our subconscious. A few examples of power statements in reference to connection that I use in my resetting ritual are:

- The purpose of my life is to honor God's light with the love I give, the gratitude I have, and the divine enthusiasm I inject into life!

- I am a limitless and boundless being, creating my new reality every day aligned with my ultimate purpose!

- Every day I tap into Source energy, being guided, reaching my full potential!

- I am full of joy, making great money, and in flow!

5. EMPTY THE CUP AND LISTEN

As our connection Element gets stronger, we yearn for more silence. We find ourselves reclusive from mundane, everyday noise, instead wishing to be in nature or a peaceful family environment. We find reading, writing, and quiet time meditative or use mindful practices as a welcome oasis within our daily lives. The soul starts yearning for nurturing. As we find ourselves in silence, the mind slowly empties our cup of all the outside noise, thoughts, and chatter we fill it up with on a daily basis. News, emails, arguments, and any other energy drain fills our cup and doesn't allow any room for blissful silence. In the silence, when we focus on our breathing, the cup is emptied and if we listen close enough, in pure surrender, the Voice of Source can be heard within our thoughts.

As I connect to my Source app, the message comes through in many ways. It can be a basic message to send out a few simple emails for work that day, a breakthrough of clarity, an acceptance of a challenge, or even nothing. But being open, surrendered to whatever may be and accepting what is, is key to being a receptor of the Voice.

As we move forward with our day after our daily connection, we'll find messages from the Voice of Source all over. We're constantly being spoken to from Source. Things we read, encounters and conversations we have, billboards we see and the never-ending list of coincidences that appear before us are all Voice connections. These are all parts of the Voice app recalculating, speaking to the "driver" to adjust course or reminding us we're going in the right direction. The more we nurture our soul, the more we will identify the messages we receive, but all this falls into our awareness. As our awareness grows, our legacy grows, and the element of connection to our Source is leverage that we can use to raise our capacity in every other element. We can rely on our connection to Source to provide strength and clarity when it comes to balancing and maintaining all our other Legacy Elements.

By fortifying these five disciplines of connection to Source, we can become a better version of ourselves today than we were yesterday. This attitude allows us to release grudges, ask and give forgiveness, be easier on our inner selves and release shames, blames, and doubts.

By aligning ourselves with our Source and our best inner selves, we're able to go to sleep at night with acceptance and satisfaction in all that we did and were that day. Considering every day could be our last day on Earth, we want to go to sleep with the knowledge that we've made strides forward toward our spiritual goals and our expanding legacy. We need to make the urgent choice to embrace our Source, so we can grow closer to a deeper understanding of what we want and need for ourselves. This is where our legacy can be dreamed, created, and established for ourselves.

Once I started accepting and surrendering, the Voice of Source got louder, the message became clearer.

CHALLENGES FOR THE READER

1. Find pockets of time during your day to shut off excess noise and thoughts. In the bath, car, office, or anywhere you spend more than five minutes a day, make a space where you're capable of turning it all off and connecting with Source as well as coming back to yourself.

2. Do a thirty-day challenge to quiet the mind and empty your cup for at least ten minutes per day. Keep a journal handy and write down whatever flows following each session.

3. Take an extended retreat to a place alone or with an organized group where you're led in cleansing your body, deep breathing exercises, or meditation. Try to share and write about your experiences with the group and as a collective. Prioritizing this group mind-set and awareness for yourself is key to jumpstarting your connection to Source!

4. Read books on spirituality. There are thousands of options, some authors I recommend are: Eckhart Tolle, Wayne Dyer, Osho, Neal Donald Walsch, and Deepak Chopra, just to name a few.

HOW THE ELEMENTS OF LEGACY INTEGRATE INTO CONNECTION

LOVE

When I was in the darkest days of my tunnel, I would start my day in the resetting ritual by meditating and connecting to my Source. I would cry and be with my Source. I loved these moments. These were my safest moments. I was cozy, warm, and protected. I was being spoken to and I was listening.

I was reminded of my great internal certainty that being connected provides for all of us. I understood that this was part of my process and I invited myself to enjoy it. Today, thankfully out of the tunnel, but so appreciative of the awareness I had during that process, my connection to Source is much different. Always warm, cozy, and protected, but now more powerful, more precise with increased certainty. **The more we get to know this divine energy the more we remember who we truly are, which is why I love connecting to my Source!**

ENERGY

The energy we give to our Source connection is by far one of the biggest leverages we will get in life and during our Legacy expansion. This idea of positive energy for leverage has resonated with me for years. Entheos, in Greek means "enthusiasm," which is a trait that I've identified with for years, but it's true root construction means "en-theos," which means "the God within." This resonated so strongly with me that I used it as a mantra for my mental mind-set, a committed goal to lead with enthusiasm, the name of my first holding company, and the name of the building I built where I currently house my offices. **The divine energy is enthusiasm, the God within.**

GROUNDED

Just because there has been a step forward with our connection to Source, where we have listened and been guided, doesn't mean we can stop there. We must still be very vigilant of our mind's thoughts and what we really listen to in our connection. Our ego is very powerful and can get in the way during our legacy expansion. This happened to me as my external results were giving me more confidence, but, for the most part, I had my Source connection on mute. This meant my external confidence for outer results totally outweighed my internal certainty that connection to Source provides. When you're in this misalignment, lessons are coming. Be grounded in your connection and double check to make sure it's not your ego stepping in and hijacking the message!

ABUNDANCE

Our spiritual process is so personal, and few speak about it. However, in my experience **when we're in alignment and find others who have the same frequency and are connected within a group at the same time, incredible things can happen.** In a recent mastermind, we went through an exercise by connecting to Source as a group and our alignment in mind-set, experience, and energy frequency was so aligned that as we shared our notes, the same words kept coming up in our different understandings. But the message was the same. We were all blessed with the same message. As our Legacy aligns with others and there is a connection to Source, the energy of Source is abundant and available to all. Altogether, now rise!

YOU

You can be dragged to church all you want but you will never expand into uncovering your true certainty, power, and peace until you do the conscious work of connecting on your own. These intangible, timeless, priceless nuggets can only be earned through the intention of wanting to know your original Source without outside influence. It's probably the most important work we have when all is said and done. It's something I wish for everyone to find on their path by consistently connecting and gratefully accepting Source in their lives.

CHAPTER SIX
LEGACY ELEMENT OF YOU

Before we give love, we must love being ourselves.

All of our legacy elements can be aligned, but you're still going to need to execute day in and day out to assure your legacy will outlive and outlast your wishes for it. At the end of days, your spouse, family, friends, and business colleagues will not be responsible for your legacy. Nobody can take care of your legacy, only you can do the work. You and only you have the opportunity, duty, and responsibility to create, rule, and expand your legacy. Are you going to take that responsibility lightly and leisurely? Or are you going to mobilize and deploy your gifts and create massive amounts of urgent action toward your goals and desires?

Ultimately, the choice for your legacy creation is in your hands alone. To continue to fulfill the balance of your Legacy Elements is an active choice, and one you must make over and over again for your legacy expansion. You must be secure in your knowledge of you to move into a space where all things are possible.

To be effective at managing *you*, we need to be able to sift through the mental and emotional noise that comes with dealing with others as well as ourselves on a day-to-day basis. There are many principles to help guide us through the maze. But the following are two fundamental laws I have found that work both simply and effectively to carve out an easy space amid all the chaos.

THE LAWS OF SHIT

1. You're going to create shit. Own it and change it.

2. Stop eating other people's shit. Decide now and allow yourself to be respected.

CREATING SHIT

One thing that makes us human is that we're all shit creators. Everyone makes mental, emotional, and physical shit, and it all stinks. From the richest to the poorest of us, the most intellectual to the least read, or from the most spiritually connected to the most superficial.

As one of my brothers used to say, it's just natural. Well, yes, that's true in a physical sense.

If we apply this methodology in a figurative sense, I would say we start creating shit in our lives at a young age, maybe four, when our ego starts getting in the way and we become somewhat aware that our needs and wants can come before others. We can say mean things, physically hurt others on purpose, and consciously manipulate.

These insensitive, ego-driven actions can be survival tactics leftover from our reptile brain and basic societal transitions that we ingrain into ourselves over time.

But as we grow older, our shit stinks more because we've allowed it to sit within ourselves and fester, instead of taking care of ourselves.

We start lying, conniving, not tending to our responsibilities, and things get rotten. We develop bad habits and even dangerous or irresponsible behaviors that create important consequences. These can deeply affect our lives over time, or even take the lives of others in an instant. We all create and have shit. Usually this shit's stuffed under a rug somewhere or left in some city we no longer live in or dumped on a relationship we don't care enough about to repair.

There's personal shit, family shit, business shit, country shit, and world shit.

The problem is that shit never goes away until you own it. Nearly everyone refuses to own all of their shit. They try to dump it on others, use excuses as to why they have it in the first place, or act as if they have never seen or smelled the pile of shit they are carrying around with them. Haven't you ever met someone who was being followed by a dump truck of shit and you have to try to act as if nothing is there? I'm sure that they know, that we know, the shit truck is following them. We can smell that messy, emotional drama from a mile away.

So we hide our shit, put on gallons of perfume or cologne to mask it, and ignore it. When people ask us about our obvious shit, we lie because we're embarrassed, ashamed, and scared that people might know that we're shit creators. No one wants to admit to their imperfections, let alone their tendencies to make and freely carry around shit.

I like to live by the simple Law of Shit, and it goes something like this: your shit may be hidden for a while, but it will float to the surface or explode until you OWN IT. Shit has a natural timer on it. It never disappears forever, because it will always linger around us, either in the ether, between our relationships, or within ourselves. What does that mean for your legacy? It's a more urgent matter now than ever that you take care of your shit, so it doesn't spread to complicate your chances for legacy growth.

The worst is, when shit explodes on you. It's mostly unexpected and usually has dire consequences. Broken relationships, corrupt identities, and financial destruction are usually inevitable. When shit floats, you know it's coming one day or another, yet you keep on ignoring it until it arrives in our faces. Then you get mad or act like a victim. Why don't you just own your shit?

Once we own our shit, there is a magic that happens. Our life becomes lighter, the hurricane barometric pressure surrounding the shit clears up and we feel stronger, cleaner. Our energy is different when we own and start cleaning up our shit.

The amazing part is we don't have to be public about owning our shit. Shit's very respectful that way. If we privately and personally admit to as well as own our shit and act in a forward manner to repair it, for the most part, the shit starts going away and clearing up. Although there is a huge benefit to owning your shit with someone else in person, it doesn't have to be that way.

So start owning your shit, and work on cleaning it up.

EATING SHIT

The other shit problem the Earth has is that we're full of shit eaters. We're constantly getting shit on us, given shit to eat, and generally having shit dropped on us. Yet, for some ungodly reason, many of us love to eat shit. Either because it's what we've learned as a child, we have a victim mentality, or because we just don't know any better. When we eat shit, we become a martyr for the shit cause, the savior for those who don't eat shit and eventually this is bad for your emotional and physical health. This is bad for you, the entire lot, and me. You aren't doing the world any favors by eating shit.

Most shit eaters are full of shit drama. They are the first ones to give you the whole run down of why their lives are surrounded by other people's shit as well as how that affects their finances, physical state, emotional balance, and spiritual connection. Which can then runoff and affect our own outlooks causing shit to bubble up within our own lives which can derail our balance of the Legacy Elements.

Those shit eaters usually feel as if they are in a shit-eating contest and have to publicize or show off how bad their shit levels are to everyone around them. We all know someone who complains about their shit and advertises their issues. Their energy is heavy, sour, and we can't hang out with them for very long. They are not someone you want to do business with, and you would generally not want to even associate with them on a regular basis, if it weren't for the fact that they are a family member or longtime friend.

We can say that shit eaters usually bring toxicity to our environment. It's amazingly expensive to be a shit eater. Your life suffers from carrying that extra stinky load. Your relationships deteriorate because nobody wants to be in the company of your shit. Your body, most likely smells and looks like shit. The amazing thing with eating shit is that it can stop at any time. All it takes is a decision! As with most things in life, you just need to say *enough is enough*. The Law of Eating Shit works once you just decide: no more. Once you decide to stop eating shit, you will!

The Second Law of Shit is that if you eat shit, you will continue to eat the same amount or a larger quantity of shit, until a decision is made to stop eating shit. I hope you too can understand the most basic principles of shit and how they apply to your life.

In summary, if you're going to eat shit, decide to stop—now.

You're going to make shit, that's okay, its natural. Own it and clean it up before it explodes, and you get shit on yourself and those you love. If we postpone dealing with our shit, we dirty up our minds, hearts, and environment so even the smallest things become emotional mountains. If we can create clear spaces in our minds for mental, emotional, and spiritual growth without the unnecessary mental garbage, we can start to think about doing things for others in an efficient manner.

A majority of life's challenges we will encounter revolve around our ability to grow in capacity and the certainty that we are up to that challenge. Perhaps the greatest challenge is whether we can create a balance between our sense of self and our growth while serving others, which is our ultimate goal as a legacy champion.

THE POWER OF LEGACY

A legacy champion is someone who's aware that they have been bestowed a legacy. They're grateful for it, regardless of all its challenges. They're conscious that they are capable of shaping and creating a legacy that they desire, and that their actions and their mind-set will define their experience. The legacy champion is one who takes urgent, massive, conscious action on a daily and long-term basis. They understand that the legacy is created in every moment, and it's not just a product, but the ongoing aggregate of a lifetime.

A legacy champion is not:

- restrained by limiting beliefs,

- of the mind-set that giving back happens only when you have accumulated significant wealth,

- waiting for others to make them happy,

- a victim to life's challenges, or

- carrying their past drama as baggage into their present.

We can often turn to the past for further guidance on how to become a proper legacy champion. Ancestor stories provide sentimental examples of legacies worth following or cautionary tales, sort of "what to do, what not to do" references. They have left their framework for us so that we can feel ourselves out in relation to their paths and see if it resonates with our energy and desires.

We must be light on our judgment because we were not in their shoes. Our ancestors executed with the best intention given their mind-set and with the resources they had on hand. At the end of the day, it all boils down to capacity. It's important to understand that the more we build our capacity, the better suited we will be to make the best decisions and have the best results.

OUR CAPACITIES

We need to close the gap within our capacity. As you increase your capacity every day, you'll start becoming a more refined version of your previous self in terms of your body, emotional intelligence, business acumen, spiritual connectedness, overall mind-set, and energy frequency. The more you update yourself, the closer you are to transcendence on a conscious level. It's a never-ending process, and the process is the point.

When we increase our capacity, our awareness and understanding of ourselves becomes deeper, refined, and precise in every sense. This is one of the reasons for life, simply to understand ourselves as our most divine and free selves. Everything else, like our limitations, fears, and judgments that we have learned and carry with us, they're costumes that keep our true selves hidden from our own consciousness. They're masks that we consistently have to learn to take off. Every time we leave behind a mask, such as fear or judgement, and are grateful for the experience, we're freer, lighter, happier. We're grateful because the release of giving up that prior unhelpful process has given us that extra certainty and inner knowledge of ourselves.

We won't necessarily be remembered for what we left behind in the physical world, but how we made people feel in their lifetimes here on Earth and through their legacy. For example, when I remember my father, I remember the emotions he brought out in me. I'm grateful for the material possessions that he might have left me, but our connection and his emotional drive are the feelings I carry with me every day. He was the person that drove me to push for excellence in life, and I'm grateful for that legacy.

My father wasn't a very communicative person. It wasn't often that we would have great in-depth conversations. But I remember the times that he made me feel safe and touched me with a fatherly, loving hand. He held me tight, sitting me on his lap at his office. Those are emotions I choose to remember him by because they last forever in me, in every cell of my body, my heart, and in my soul. It's not even what he said. It's the way that his words or grunts or touch made me feel inside. What I remember is his energy, more than anything.

In the end, nothing is yours. It's your choice whether or not you spread your message on multiple channels to those around you who you can influence, whether your legacy is positive or negative. If you don't share your experiences with other people, you're discounting other people from their possible memories and experiences with you. If your capacity is low, your discounting everyone in your life from having the very best experience with you that you're capable of producing. If you add to that capacity every day, imagine the positive refinement of the experience of yourself others will have of you as you continue to grow in capacity.

The average male in the United States lives until age seventy-nine, and about fifty-five of those years are materially productive. How old are you and how much time do you have left based on these statistics? What are you going to do with your remaining years? With those limited years of impact on the world, you can't have more time, but you can work to live intentionally without distractions to make the most of your time. By learning to compound our time, live with purpose, and give our hearts and our minds to the right places, we can multiply our legacy into an impact that's never forgotten. When you put in the work to better yourself, you're ensuring that any future conflicts will be negotiable and workable in the face of your self-worth within the reach of your legacy cannon.

CHALLENGE TO THE READER

WORST CRITIC LETTER EXERCISE

We're all our own worst critics. One way of accessing and accepting our judgements of ourselves, so we can fulfill and reach our maximum capacity, is by writing ourselves the opposite of a love letter. Instead, we'll write a hate letter. Write to yourself like you're a troll. Troll yourself. Write all your self-criticisms and call out all your soft, weak, or vulnerable points. Write them out and then read your letter out loud. You might even share it with a few loved ones.

After you've told yourself what your biggest fears are and what your biggest weak spots are, those burdens become lighter. You get all that negativity off your chest by bringing it out into the open. You name the eight-hundred-pound elephant that's in the room, that way it's a lot easier to stop feeding that elephant.

Once we understand all those limitations, that what we've put to paper is in our heads and not in other people's minds, we understand that those fears are the emergency breaks that keep us from going forward. We keep on wondering why our car doesn't run smoothly but haven't dealt with our own self-judgements or negativity that are giving us a bumpy, negative ride. Those are the fears that hold us back. By releasing them into the world, they lose their power over us and cease to exist.

HOW THE ELEMENTS OF LEGACY INTEGRATE INTO YOU

LOVE

Loving yourself sounds so egotistical. The other day I was having a discussion with my wife and she was telling me how she felt disconnected from me, as if she wasn't a priority. I admitted that she hadn't been one in the past few days and I apologized for it. I told her my priority right then was me. She didn't let me finish explaining before making the "I knew you were that selfish" face, but I finally told her that if I wasn't a priority, I wouldn't have anything to give her, the kids, or the upcoming two intense weeks of work and still be healthy. Yes, I used to be super-egotistical in the bad way. I used to manipulate situations to get what I wanted out of my relationships, so I could party and slack off. But now I use my self-love for myself to egotistically have the capacity to serve others. **If I don't feed myself, I will not be able to serve anyone else.**

ENERGY

Legacy creation, ruling, and expansion requires the energy of You. Legacy requires sacrifice, boldness, awareness, and detailed intention. To withstand our constant stretch of life requires industrial quantities of energy. The good news is that **the more aligned we are, the more our energy recharges and recreates itself,** much like an electric car battery being charged by the friction of tires and brakes. It all adds up.

However, when our energy level dips, we will lose our capacity and ability for Legacy expansion. We must be mindful of the energy that's put out there by us, but mostly aware of the energy that's taken from us, because of our lack of awareness. These energy losses can be draining people who take our energy, sedation with substance abuse, or losing ourselves in a nonproductive TV series. But if we're going to let this energy drain happen consciously, then we should have a disciplined plan for recharging our energy batteries. For example, if I know I'm going to a dinner party and will have some drinks, I make the mental note of committing to waking up and pushing myself harder in my workout the next day, because of that misalignment that having a drink will cause in my energy level. **Every energy drain has an opportunity cost and should be replaced with another form of positive energy to even the scales.**

GROUNDED

Nothing communicates trust to others more than being vulnerable. This is leadership 101. This gets a room of people you don't know to trust your word and intention through conscious and grounded sharing of experiences. When we can appreciate all the temporary setbacks and tough times enough to share them so others can learn and grow as well, it's worth telling our story. Your story matters when told from a place of humility and with the intention of helping others. As I prepare for speeches or even as I write this book, I remember the words of my wife, who told me the night before a TEDx speech I made, "If you can reach at least one person that listens to your message, you have been successful." She also reminds me of the famous quote: "To give without remembering and receive without forgetting."

ABUNDANCE

The more we understand that we're energetic, timeless, limitless beings and start to find increasing examples of that in our lives, that there are no coincidences and that we're guided, the easier it is to fathom an abundant You. **We have to be crazy and literally "lose" our minds to find our true nature and Divine Certainty.** This is because we have generations of limiting conditioning left in our bodies and brains that we have learned on Earth through human systems and programming. There is so much dormant DNA in us waiting to be uncovered and put to work. I invite you all to start uncovering the inner abundance of You.

CONNECTION

What is more powerful: someone who's connected to Source, or someone that's empty and feels as if they have no foundation to face life's challenges? I've lived both realities and chose the former, because I knew with complete certainty that **we're portals for divine energy if we so choose to align ourselves to the correct reality where anything can be achieved.** How do we know we're connecting more to Source? For me, my experience has to come with clarity, surrender, and acceptance. It's a feeling of being lighter, but stronger and a sense of being that equips you to best handle your life. Like all the best emotions such as love, happiness, and gratitude, being connected allows us to flow and feel lighter as well as freer.

CHAPTER SEVEN
BREAKING THROUGH THE TUNNEL

Every human will confront multiple tunnels
in their life. We have to traverse those
tunnels and come out alive or die inside them.
Surviving our tunnels are our greatest gifts!

TUNNELS ARE UNIVERSAL PAIN

E very human will confront multiple tunnels in their life. This
can be similar to a mid-life crisis, but it's a complete breakdown
of everything that we know and understand in our lives.
In order to become the ultimate legacy champion for our family and
for our legacy, we have to traverse those tunnels and either come
out alive or die inside them. When we die in the tunnel, we have
succumbed to our fears, shames, and pains, and they will consume us
from the inside out for the rest of our days. While in the tunnel, we
doubt everything. Unless we become slippery like Teflon and develop
an internal certainty that we're more than all of our doubt, then we

will not survive. Our tunnels exist to test our Legacy Elements and all the work we've put into balancing our lives thus far. We become true legacy champions when we can anticipate and circumnavigate the possible tunnels that will crop up in our lives with ease and self-awareness.

Our tunnels are a process of facing a pain so great that it either consumes us or we come out on the other side before it overcomes us. It's a pain that tests our Legacy Elements at their core. We typically encounter a handful of various tunnels that lead us to defining our legacy in every major stage of our lives: as a teen, in college, our thirties or fourties, empty nesters, and then our golden years. The tunnels can and do include: addiction, past mental or physical abuses, divorce, loss of a loved one, financial disruption, spiritual vacuums, or personal health issues. If you're from a country like Nicaragua, as I am, revolution is something that can appear multiple times in your lifetime. Our tunnels are significant life challenges that we will all encounter at some point or another during our lifetime.

THE RULES OF A TUNNEL

- Tunnels represent significant pain, struggles, and fears we must overcome going through our journeys to becoming legacy champions.

- We must move forward embracing self-forgiveness and reducing our self-judgment of our current situation. You are the only one who can save yourself, so judging the new you is of no use.

- It's not safer to stay in the tunnel even if we can't see what we're working toward on the other side. Always keep moving—staying put will lead to "death in the tunnel."

- Only by sticking to our Legacy Element rituals can we fight through our tunnel; they will offer us a lifeline when nothing else will anchor us. They will provide the necessary checkpoints of light and oxygen along the way.

- Fear is our fuel—use it to power out of the tunnel.

MY TUNNEL EXPERIENCE

My tunnel was related to one of my biggest identities I created for myself: a successful entrepreneur. I created a business that grew too fast and became too big without developing the skills I needed to correctly lead it into a successful future. My precision, per se, to run the business was off by a few millimeters, and over time that led me astray within the business.

When I struggled to keep my Legacy Elements in balance I suffered for my inability to keep all the pieces moving in positive, forward directions. Not only did my work suffer while I was in the tunnel, my family nest egg suffered greatly, and I put my family at risk while our income hung in the balance. A weight of guilt settled on my shoulders and I fought to get out from under that pressure.

In order to survive and fix what had been broken, I had to let go of valuable people and close operations that my team and I had invested a lot of energy to create. That's when I knew there was no going back; I could only go forward and hope to salvage what was crumbling around me. I tasted failure in every taste bud. There was one day when we had to let go of twenty-seven people in the same day, in five different countries. I personally had to let go of five people in person that day, some of my closest team members with whom I had the most emotional investments.

My assistant of sixteen years, who saw me get married, who was there at the birth of all three of my children, and who was both a mother figure as well as an emotional and administrative support system, had to be let go as the ax fell. That was an excruciatingly tough day for the entire organization. The guilt and shame I carried around on my shoulders was unbearable and I promptly drowned my emotions in alcohol.

The world I'd built was crumbling, and the scattered rubble of fear, uncertainty, and pain was blocking me from moving in any direction. I was left with a total lack of clarity on how to get out of my quagmire. When I brought home the emergency package to fix my business and presented it to my wife, it was too late. My failure had become complete. I tried to negotiate my way out from the corner that I'd unknowingly backed myself into for over three years, but there was no going back.

Eventually, I had to shut down a large portion of my business. The ordeal of closing operations, capitulating the market positions to competitors who I'd fought against for years, letting go of wonderful people, and losing millions of dollars of our family's nest egg was unendingly painful. I was living through failure in every cell of my body. I had to accept the inevitable defeat and destroy an important identity I had created for myself. An identity that defined me for so long was gone. I was lost, without an anchor.

After the business I had envisioned and created was dismantled, every morning I would wake up feeling as if there was a hole in my stomach. I'd have an unending heat in my head, neck, and back that would stiffen through my shoulders until they ached all the time. The physical process was on par with the worst of my emotional wounds as I fought to stay afloat.

My survival instinct was working overtime. My reptile brain was on fire. I didn't want to get out of bed and confront reality because it was safer to stay hiding in the fetal position rather than dealing with the uncertainty of my future. Meanwhile, my teams were looking to me for answers. They would ask me where we were going, what we needed to do in the wake of all this chaos. How was I supposed to answer their questions, when I didn't have the most basic of answers? The worst was when they would bring back the rumors swirling about our business to me and ask for my input. I was helpless and unsure in a sea of their questions; leading wasn't second nature to me and it wasn't something I felt equipped to do anymore. I didn't have an answer for them.

Probably the worst professional challenge I've ever faced was giving my word and not being able to deliver on it. Not knowing your direction and asking your team to still do their best work every day is a pain I don't wish on any business owner. But as I crawled through the tunnel, I learned to acknowledge, face, and own my struggles, knowing if I shed light on the pain that I was facing that fear would no longer control me. To become the legacy champion I was meant to be, I had to rise above my pain and fear in order to come back to my Legacy Element baseline to begin serving myself as well as others.

SYMPTOMS OF THE TUNNEL

A sinking sense of awareness rolled through my body while going through this defining, gut-wrenchingly mental, emotional, and physical process, as well as a huge upheaval in my life. There couldn't possibly be a single upside. But that's where I grasped the value of being in the tunnel. Despite the crippling levels of awareness and uncertainty that made my brain ache on a day-to-day basis, that same pain that defined me could be used as a positive awareness tool to learn how not to make this mistake again. By being completely aware of everything that was happening to me—the decisions I was making, as well as the physical and emotional connections within myself—my painful sense of awareness allowed me to look forward to the end of my tunnel.

That growing, starkly painful awareness also opened me up to understanding that I wasn't alone in my pain. There are so many people that go through their tunnel at the same time. Our friends and family, a woman walking down the street, a man buying coffee in front of us at the coffee shop, they're all around us. Yet, we have no idea. When I was in my tunnel, there were about half a dozen friends or family members going through their tunnel at the same time. It's life. We're going to get completely uncomfortable. We're going to question ourselves to the core of what we're made of in order to grow our capacity to eventually thrive. Our capacity to expand will be tested, and that's why we're given these tunnels in the first place—to see if we're consciously capable of expanding to make changes needed for our futures.

There are two options: (1) either we continue to be tested in our own personal tunnel until we die there, or (2) we choose to expand beyond our limits in order to break free once and for all.

There are two options: (1) either we continue to be tested in our own personal tunnel until we die there, or (2) we choose to expand beyond our limits in order to break free once and for all.

While in the tunnel, we will be rocked with fears. These fears will consume us, literally, until we start having physical symptoms that spread internally throughout our bodies in a physiological response. Symptoms can arise in various ways such as night sweats, anxiety, panic attacks, fear of people, depression, isolation, staring off into space, or hives. But fear doesn't have to be our master. Fear can only control us as much as we allow it.

Instead, we can transform our fear into the fuel that propels us forward into positive actions. Each positive action is a step in the right direction; each choice to use our fear as fuel breaks our limiting walls and executes a change in our reality going forward with our lives. Fear is like jet fuel. It either powers us to amazing heights extremely efficiently, or it blows us up. Only we can decide our fate, if we're aware enough during the process.

If we expand and come out alive on the other end, we'll be blessed with a new life and complete clarity, an internal certainty that we walk with on a day-to-day basis. Specifically, we gain the certainty that can be felt through a renewed sense of peace, enthusiasm for new opportunities, and industrial amounts of gratitude. Our fears are no longer our kryptonite.

ESCAPING THE TUNNEL: AN INTEGRATED PROCESS

So how do we pull ourselves out of the tunnel? How do we reach that seemingly elusive internal **certainty**? Our personal Legacy Element rituals gives us our freedom by allowing us to wake up every morning with a steady blueprint of how we're going to stay on track for legacy creation. Every day I did my Legacy Elements rituals. I gave myself my space. I wrote in my journal, and I consciously went through the tunnel studying, feeling, and taking notes. This gave me the strength to power through the process. As the saying goes, "while driving through hell, don't stop and take a look around—power through it." If we have nothing else, we have ourselves and our rituals feed into our slightly muddied but nevertheless strong understanding of what we're capable of within ourselves as we relate to the rest of the world. Our rituals keep us grounded so we can regain clarity during the tough times and confront truths that we might not want to look at in the light of day.

In order to change our results, we have to be willing to address our weaknesses, mastering the art of being okay with failure, and giving into the emotional pain we've been avoiding in our lives. One of the hardest things for people to wrap their heads around is that reality is physically based, separated by time, and completely individualized. However, when we have experiences where time disappears, we feel the emotion of being connected to all humanity. We finally digest that we're one with all of life, God, and creation. Then our previous limits are shattered. This is where spiritual expansion takes place, in the overwhelming tsunami of love, acceptance, and peace that sweeps us away.

While going through my process, my connection with my Source was amplified. I was reading books on spirituality and many things became clear to me. I had to:

- accept my reality and take responsibility for my situation,

- surrender and trust the process I was going through, and

- detach myself from any outcomes I had in my head for the future.

I began to identify these three steps, which are purely conscious. They have nothing to do with outside circumstances, but I consciously identified them as a code to power me through the tunnel. So those three decisions had to be aligned in order for me to find any sort of awareness or clarity, while also sticking to my rituals and staying on the path of keeping to my micro- and macro-balance throughout all elements of the legacy system.

Discovering this process consciously, however, is very personal and must be relearned cognitively, emotionally, and physically. I say "relearned" because we all come onto this earth knowing freedom, peace, and happiness. That wonder and amazement of discovering ourselves as babies, as a spirit, we unlearn as we grow up and bring drama, violence, and the human condition into our lives. We're taught that we're separate from everyone else. Although we must each go through our own individual process, we're connected and part of something much greater if we allow ourselves to relearn that truth.

One of the important parts of our relearning is Mother Nature. When we're alone in Mother Nature, we feel connected, transported, and completely alive. Whether it's being in a forest or being on a mountaintop, there's always a sense of intimate connection with nature and a spiritual experience with the view.

About ten years ago, I was in Aspen, Colorado, and I went to Taylor Pass, which is above the timberline. It's in the tundra, and approximately twelve thousand feet above sea level. The view of snow-capped Rockies until the edge of the horizon was so profound. That was one of the moments in life where I said, "There is a God." It was so spectacular. The funny thing about nature is that the "now" is nearly always there. The sense of being present in the now is just there, experienced through being there, with all of its infinite granular ecosystems. It keeps you present. That view is never going to go away. So that sense of being in the present moment should be inside of you all the time, and that's what we have to relearn as humans.

THE POST-TUNNEL EVOLUTION

There are several stages of moving through the tunnel by intentioned physical, emotional, spiritual, and meditative practices. But the simple answer to getting out is to never stop pushing forward with those rituals. The rituals keep us grounded amidst chaos. The worst mistake we make is when we stop our constructive habits on the second day. It's clear we may miss a day, but two days straight is sacrilege. If we've decided we can't stay in the tunnel and were trying to build up new habits, we can't become flexible with our discipline.

In discipline, we find freedom. When we're faced with our biggest challenges, we will depend and revert to our core fundamentals. Which fundamentals drive us? Let's remember the *Karate Kid*: "Wax on. Wax off." Those rituals are the ones he questioned and hated the most, but in the end he developed the discipline until he was aware of the refinement needed to master the basics. Those rituals saved his hide in the big fight at the end of the movie.

Likewise, although we have the urge to sedate with pills, drugs, alcohol, sex, TV, and video games to avoid our pain, we will never find internal certainty in ourselves or expand until we face our deeper issues. We must face what we have become—our fears, and ourselves. Remember Luke Skywalker going into the swamp and facing his deepest fears? Only then was he able to refine his Jedi powers.

If you fear it, then you must. We're naturally programmed to avoid uncomfortable emotions that can serve as our light to see out of the tunnel, purely because of our propensity to feed our own egos and our prehistoric needs for survival. We don't think we can survive our fears because we're programmed that way, but we can reprogram ourselves, rather than feeding our egos.

If you fear it, then you must.

When we feed our egos, we build a wall around our sense of awareness both within ourselves and with the outside world. Feeding our ego gives us external confidence that's built on things that we temporarily rent and shift with time, giving us a false sense of pride or happiness (our booming business, our abs, our attractive, young girlfriend, et al.). But our ego is not truly who we are as a person. It's the titles, identities, and a fulfillment of the mass marketing machine that holds no actual authenticity to the self. It's only a matter of time until these fictional realities are tested or destroyed. As those falsehoods come crashing down and we're left with the rituals and disciplines that we've honed in over time that give us purpose, clear the way for our future, and represent our goals. We can hold the space for our inner reality while rebuilding a new outer reality that fits our legacy mind-set.

The more fears I had, the more I would dive into myself: working out, reading, writing, meditating, being quiet and still, creating magic moments with my family, crying, speaking to myself. I was my own guru. Clarity started coming into my life as a plan of action. Decisions, choices, they were up to me. By accepting a plan of action and being at peace with my best efforts, I went into a zone.

However, this clarity process didn't happen alone. I surrounded myself with an executive coach, a mastermind, a thinking partner, a mentor and many other friends, professionals and especially my family that gave me their time, experiences, and energy to support me. I'm ever grateful to all of them for their love, support, and positive energy.

With their help when challenges would come up, I would overcome the obstacles. I started getting momentum because my energy shifted every day that I showed up and did the work for myself. Of course, I didn't come out unscathed. There was loss and pain. But what I learned and developed was an internal peace and certainty. This was worth one hundred times more than what I lost while crawling through the mud to the other side. Surviving the tunnel was the catalyst that made me decide to write this book.

When we're in fear, we either react in fight, flight, or freeze response. We must be aware and conscious of what is happening to us when these situations arise, so we don't fall into misalignment and stay in survival mode. If we can't align ourselves with the three steps that I mentioned before and be aware of what we're doing to ourselves by our mental and emotional processes, it will be difficult to expand beyond basic survival techniques, much less legacy creation and expansion.

By being aware of how to break through your tunnels you can clean your emotional and mental slates to move forward with your best intentions.

What is your biggest trauma? Where did your fears reside as a child? Mine were getting robbed and seeing my parents fight over money. Those fears translated into my life, as I couldn't take care of others as a responsible provider without financial stability. I didn't have my first child until I was thirty-one, but I had "children" to take care of since I was twenty-two—my team members were my responsibility, or that was the mind-set I had then. Eventually, there was a time when meeting the payroll wasn't an issue. But when I hit the tunnel with my business and our family nest egg lost millions, I was swimming in my biggest trauma all over again.

It wasn't until that moment that I realized a few important breakthroughs:

1. MY WIFE SUPPORTED ME NO MATTER THE RESULT.

There were a few occasions where I was nervous, embarrassed, and downright going to the well again because nothing had worked. I was afraid of failing and didn't have a clear plan to execute yet, but I had to keep betting on myself. My wife would encourage me to pick myself up and keep on fighting. She would say: "You need to change these results. I trust your decisions and am willing to do whatever we need to do to support you."

To actually hear as well as feel her support and acceptance defined many moments for a man who wants to lead others, especially his family, into a successful legacy. She was there for me, through thick and thin. Thank you, Amor!

2. MY CHILDREN WOULD LOVE ME NO MATTER THE LACK OF LUXURIES.

One night during the tunnel, I was with my eldest son. We were in bed, had just prayed, and I was writing in my journal. I was in a fear and scarcity mind-set, worried about the unknown in our futures. I asked him, "Would you still love me if we didn't take any trips this year and we had to cut back on the luxuries we have?" He looked up at me and told me, "That's the dumbest question I've ever heard you ask! Of course, Dad. I'll always love you."

Although sometimes we think our children can be the source of unconditional love, there are times when we need to be sure, especially when we're overflowing with doubt. Not being able to provide the experiences that I want to give them made me afraid I'd lose their love as well. But that was only fear and ego talking; of course they had my back. Thanks Buddy Champ!

3. I WAS SO MUCH MORE THAN WHAT DEFINED ME ON THE OUTSIDE.

The last breakthrough was during my resetting ritual, when I was crying my eyes out through my pain and lack of clarity. After a few minutes, my swollen eyes looked to the mirror and a peace fell over me. All of this noise, all of these emotions and this storm did not define me. It only refined me. I knew that even if I was alone, naked, and not loved by anyone with my material possessions gone, I was a son of God and God's divine power resided in me, just like any other individual. That allowed me to find my internal certainty and not let any temporary setback in my external confidence affect my being.

These three breakthroughs, as basic as they may seem, are not simple when your identity and external confidence is being tested and destroyed. We need these solid steps to help us find a new foundation on which we are able to construct a new post-tunnel era for our lives. Only then can we move forward with our best intentions to better serve our communities, our friends and family, and ultimately, the world.

There's no time in our day-to-day existence to accept or acknowledge our past or future fears, so by using the following meditation we release our pain and destroy time in the process. Pain is important and necessary to move us toward our best selves, and fear is a motivator that spurs us into action in reaction to our fears. Humans are motivated by pleasure and the fear of pain. Unfortunately, we usually have our biggest breakthroughs through pain motivation. So, pain is the best form of feedback.

Physical pain will tell us when we're out of shape. Emotional pain will tell us that drama in our relationships is not the way we want to conduct ourselves or what we want for our future. Financial pain will tell us we need to expand our skillset. Spiritual pain will rock our core, our mind, our heart and our body, until we learn better. Pain is extremely efficient, because we want it to stop immediately.

There's a beauty in becoming comfortable with our discomfort.

However, if we sedate, smother, or become oblivious to our pain, then our pain will only come back stronger. There's a beauty in becoming comfortable with our discomfort, in order to obtain the power to confront our tunnels by taking the right steps toward the light and unleashing our urgency to crawl through the mud to the other side.

CHALLENGES FOR THE READER

A MEDITATION EXERCISE TO MOVE FORWARD

As an exercise to sort through your present, past, and future, consider conducting this meditation, which I've done on several occasions to bring me a sense of inner peace and unwavering gratitude.

- Start by envisioning a younger version of yourself, a version of yourself as you are now, and a future self. To the left of you are versions of yourself ending with you as a baby, one for every year of your life. To the right of you are all the versions of you in the future, until you're at your last year in old age. It's like peeking into two circus mirrors.

- Then visualize bringing forward yourself as a young child, for me that's around eleven years old. I chose that age because it was when I was scared that I was moving to a new country. Now have your younger self step forward and stand in front of you and then call on an older version of yourself, say seventy years old, to meet face-to-face with the young you.

- From there I have the old me tell the young me that it's okay, everything is going to be fine. That all the fears that I have from the past, I don't need to carry with me any longer. The older you knows how to comfort the younger you from his fears. This dialogue will allow the younger you to be at peace. The little scared you that is still within you, gains peace.

- Then visualize both sides of yourself going back into line. Every age and incarnation of your past and future selves, they all converge into yourself as you are now. Into who you are right now, at this moment.

- Those fears you carried for years should be gone or at least greatly reduced. The idea of time should be compacted because you have built up the capacity to go into the past as well as the future and be at peace with yourself at whichever point in your life isn't working. Surprisingly, those past and future selves are carried with you into the present and so will their sense of healing.

As an additional exercise, your present self can ask future you for advice. Listen to the answers already residing within you.

CHAPTER EIGHT

SERVING YOUR INTENTIONS

We are servants and knowing who we are serving in this moment is the clarity one desires. Serve with humility, serve by listening, serve with passion, but mostly serve with love.

SERVING MY COMMUNITY

During a visit to our condo at the beach, which was one of our first family investments as well as a second home, we cherished the place where our kids could grow up living a beach life on the weekends and being connected to nature. This was a community and a way of life we wanted to preserve for our kids' legacy so they could have a better appreciation for nature, our ecosystem, and life's more simple pleasures outside of video games and modern technology. My intentions were to show them a different side to life, but on the other side of that coin comes life's little disruptions to my pure intentions. While we were visiting, we noticed that during the rainy seasons heavy rains would overflow the estuary, dumping into the bay and bring a lot of garbage with it. The underdeveloped and underfunded municipal effort was no match for the bad trash management habits within the local communities.

Instead of enjoying our family time and embracing nature, we would arrive for our relaxation to find the beach littered with garbage. We would spend hours picking up all types of trash because we couldn't stand the mess and didn't see anyone else taking care of it. After identifying this negative aspect of our new community, my anger had accumulated as a result of spending literally hours at a time of being a good example.

I got really pissed. Sometimes we have to be driven to anger to decide to change a current reality. I decided enough was enough. I got in touch with the local community education non-governmental organizations (NGOs) that worked in the area and led beach cleanup efforts. It took a few months between my company, two NGOs, and the local municipal authorities, but we were able to launch a full-time beach cleanup on the country's most iconic beach and tourism destination. For eighteen months, we had three full-time beachcombers, which created employment, a clean beach, and promoted solid waste education in the local businesses and to hundreds of young students.

During this time, more than ninety thousand pounds of solid waste was accounted for by our efforts. Thousands of dollars were put into the local economy through recycling revenue and the local businesses bought into the culture, as well as the importance of maintaining a clean beach. Today, the trash culture in our community has completely changed. The municipal authorities have their own beach combers, the local business community became a leader in leading by example, the youth of the town understand how to handle solid waste and they, in turn, teach their parents.

Through this great experience, I gained an understanding that anger and rage can be turned into something positive. I was able to serve my intentions to my community and make an impact on the world at large because I understood how to bring about positive and intentional change. By remaining aware of my capabilities within myself and not succumbing to my frustration, instead using it as enacting power to move forward with change, I became better for my new choice. I stretched myself and grew my capacity to solve issues that affected many more people than just my family or myself. To truly serve our intentions, we must understand by doing so that our actions are for the greater good. Only then can we make the changes needed in ourselves to lead as legacy champions to further our cause as we move forward with life.

Many years later, I have the pleasure of visiting our beach without worrying about the garbage problem or how trash would impact my family, who personally benefited from the community's shift in understanding recycling. But the big winner was the environment and the entire community. Garbage still is, and will always be, a big issue, but now clean beach culture has been instilled and new leaders are picking up the baton.

After this experience, I was invited by one of the NGOs to be on their board where I remained active for over six years. This led to more work with conservation, including reforestation. This is a simple example of what channeling our outrage into a more positive action can do to possibly impact many people, and especially impact our sense of self as we continue to expand in all areas of our lives. I consider this a direct example of living in line with our Legacy Elements to preserve our future for our children to the best of our ability.

However, serving our intentions is only one step in the three-step process to becoming a true legacy champion.

The Three Stages to Being a Legacy Champion

1.   Create your legacy intentionally.

2.   Rule your legacy urgently.

3.   Expand your legacy with awareness.

1. CREATE YOUR LEGACY INTENTIONALLY.

Each one of us starts our legacy process by being legacy creatives. We work creatively with our desires and dreams to create a vision of what our legacy could be in the future.

Our first step in the legacy process is to begin organizing our thoughts, our energy, our words, and our actions in order to begin our conscious process of creating a legacy. We can document this process by writing vision statements and goals for each role we play in our lives. I have a vision for ten roles I play in my life and I title them with emotionally charged words that get me enthusiastic about those experiences. I suggest writing a vision for yourself to work toward in one hundred days, one year, and so on until your ultimate vision, so you can easily identify when you're having success and coming close to reaching your goals.

We start taking concerted, intentional action with every Legacy Element to advance it forward. We understand that our time is limited, and in general we're limited in our resources as we begin the legacy creation process. Faith on its own rarely manifests, we must take concerted action to become creators of our desires.

Part of that first step is also associating with the proper people to help us advance our desire in each element. This may be the point where we decide to disassociate ourselves from people who are not aligned with our Legacy Elements and overall vision for our lives. We start cutting off the drag that we have on our Legacy Elements in order to be more efficient and lean. Proper association of like-minded souls is key to garner the skillset, mind-set, and support to create your ultimate legacy.

2. RULE YOUR LEGACY URGENTLY.

The second stage involves ruling our legacy. Ruling our legacy consists of putting forth intentional, every day work in each Legacy Element to work toward consistency in each area. As long as we're consistent in our microbalance for aligned daily actions, then we're progressing forward. We can look at 1 percent improvements daily. Over a year's time we will have compounded time and should have increased our capacity threefold, at least, during a year.

This intentional progress is where most people crumble in their process. They have neither practiced, nor prepared for doing this type of legacy work every day. When we're building a legacy, the process requires sacrifice, pain and becoming comfortable with being uncomfortable. I wasn't like this before, but I found so much value in the practice that building myself up to become balanced became my discipline, my freedom, and separated me from the pack. Not in an egotistical sense, where I'm better than anyone else, but I'm more focused on my priorities and my future.

These are my priorities. I'm into my legacy, period.

MEASURING LEGACY AWARENESS

Part of facilitating—and the nerdy fun of this discipline—is the measurement of our aligned daily actions. The more precise we get in every area of our lives, the more capacity building we can attain for our future. Capacity building, as well as the results of those positive actions, acts as our intuitive dashboard and reality check. We know when we're intentionally putting in the effort to remain on course to achieve our dreams. With our exact measurements, we get to celebrate ourselves and share our success with others.

This intentional work awareness also means we get to adjust our course as soon as we get off course. Modern airplanes, when flying due north on autopilot, only are flying due north 7 percent of the time. The rest of the trip is achieved by tiny, precise, constant adjustments within the system that we don't feel as a passenger to remain on course. Building a legacy and keeping ourselves on our path toward achievement is much the same. A constant assessment of small, aligned, strategic changes in every area of our lives to build toward our goals until flying toward success becomes a routine habit. It's a game of precision and feedback that becomes a passion for an advanced ruler of his legacy.

Ruling your legacy means taking responsibility and owning it— your awareness and acceptance of your various roles as a leader, entrepreneur, community leader, spouse, parent, child, sibling, and friend. You own your roles completely with pride. However, you don't carry out that responsibility because you've merely taken up a title within your workplace, family, and circle of friends. But you honor that title because you're serving others. You serve your responsibilities with passion, poise, and presence. You constantly set a new standard as you step up to the next level of capacity.

3. EXPAND YOUR LEGACY WITH AWARENESS.

The third level of building a legacy involves legacy expansion. Legacy champions are constantly expanding, growing, and transcending. When we're most confronted by our dark challenges, that's when our light shines and we can find it in ourselves to rise above our current limitations. This is where our external confidence is exchanged for internal certainty. We find more meaning in life, as well as more clarity, when our connection to our Source grows more profound. However, our journey is a day-by-day process and reaching for perfection is not the ultimate destination. Progress is the name of the game and it's how to stay sane. We're becoming masters at refining our legacies and each day appreciating the opportunity to extract lessons to add to our craft. We're not defined by what we do, but refined by how we do it.

> **Progress is the name of the game and it's how to stay sane.**

> **We're not defined by what we do, but refined by how we do it.**

Legacy expansion means we impact others around us. We impact not only on an economic level, but also on an intangible, spiritual or mental level by shifting others' energy to be aligned with the frequency of their own undiscovered power. It becomes clear the process of legacy expansion is not about us anymore. It's how we serve others, how we make them feel, and how we lead them to discover their own path.

When we're expanding our legacy, we bring value to every interaction and more value to the table than anyone else. Our work, awareness, and consciousness are becoming next level and invaluable. By creating an example of a life well lived, we're able to elevate the consciousness of those we impact in our lives. We're no longer operating from a one-person position, as many have aligned with the message of legacy expansion, and are contributing with their own legacies.

We have become legacy champions as well as champions of our legacy. This is the shift in consciousness that as individuals will impact the world to create the best outcome for our lives, legacies, and collective future generations. Once we've implemented the three stages of becoming our best version of a legacy champion through creation, ruling, and expansion, we can work toward seeking a balance within our legacy that will reap rewards for all those who follow behind us.

WHAT

Create intentionally by transcending your past.

HOW

Rule urgently by balancing your present.

WHY

Expand with awareness by serving for generations.

CHALLENGES FOR THE READER

1. What are you good at and what do you like to do? Find an organization locally with a need for your skillset and contribute your time. Establish a goal in annual volunteer hours to give and achieve those hours.

2. What makes you so mad in the world because it's not working and is causing pain? Get involved in the solution for the root cause of the problem. Campaigning against things is fine and dandy, but until we understand the functioning of the subconscious and that it doesn't understand negatives, we'll see it's more powerful to "protect what we love, rather than destroy what we hate."[9]

3. Heroes are everywhere, usually right under our noses. For me it was my wife, who for over a decade has supported and organized annual fundraising events for an at-risk young girls' home, who is on the board of our children's school, and who contributes to many other community programs. She works hard, and the impact of her work is important. Find a hero right under your nose and recognize them, take notes, and then raise your game.

---

9   *Star Wars: The Last Jedi*. Directed by Rian Johnson. Performed by Mark Hamill. United States: Walt Disney Studio Motion Pictures, 2017. Film.

CHAPTER NINE

LEGACY OF BALANCE

Whether we fall into misalignment isn't
the question. It's how long it takes us
to be conscious and align again.

MICRO-BALANCE AND MACRO-BALANCE

B y building a concrete legacy and mastering our lives, we don't
have to split our time into four quarters every day in order to
tackle our spiritual, mental, emotional, and physical goals. Our
lives are about balance as much as we struggle to maintain the balance
between our Legacy Elements on a daily basis. So I believe that work/
life balance can be summarized and simplified if broken apart into
the concepts of micro-balance and macro-balance. Each concept has
an overall effect on our ability to juggle our legacy mind-set and
strive to set a positive example for the future with each choice we
make in the present.

Micro-balance is the act of consciously touching on every one of our Legacy Elements every day. We may be on a business trip away from home, but we're still able to exercise, meditate, FaceTime our family, and give a street peddler a smile and a compliment on top of excelling and investing in a twelve-hour day at work. Even though one Legacy Element may have been prioritized that day, the others were touched, leaving us emotionally, psychologically, and physically in balance and in control.

Macro-balance is having a proper mix of all six Legacy Elements over the long term. Over a one- or two-year period is an ideal timeline where we've seen excellent results and have honed our habits, rituals, and disciplines to achieve our goals in all of the Legacy Elements. This isn't instituting an expectation of perfection, but rather a growing awareness of keeping ourselves in line with our personal goals to achieve our best self, as well as the habits that reinforce our best behavior. Simply by forming a habit of integrating every stage of the legacy system, every day, we can hone our consciousness until being our best self isn't a conscious effort. By resolving to align ourselves with all six Legacy Elements, we can consciously create a stronger precedent for the long-term.

Find the Balance by Coming Back to Center.

1. Define misalignment.

2. Develop a routine.

3. Actively take back your time.

DEFINE MISALIGNMENT.

The more alertness and recognition play a role in our day-to-day lives, the stronger we will grow over time. For instance, our health and physical shape has improved, our business has been growing by leaps and bounds, allowing us to focus on our unique abilities. Our key relationships are much more fulfilling as well as fun, and we feel a deep tranquility inside. All the pieces are in place to create a positive, mindful legacy, which will in turn bring even more abundance into our lives.

Additionally, our levels of gratitude increase because of the renewed blessings in our lives. While drawing on our awareness and intention to seek balance, we compound time on a conscious level. We become aware of our moments in misalignment, quickly reverting back to our center so we don't discount others experience of you.

If I fall into misalignment, I'd much rather do it ten times a day for four minutes each, than one time for forty minutes. Being able to realign strengthens your muscles. Falling into misalignment for an extended period affects an entire day and is much more detrimental to your entire psyche and mind-set in general.

Not until we dominate and consciously work on both the micro-balance and macro-balance will we begin to achieve amazing compounding results. Micro- and macro-balance within our Legacy Elements and our lives are interrelated and interdependent, we must focus on all of them to unleash our full potential. While raising our awareness and working to better ourselves, we raise the bar on our most limiting Legacy Elements. Our acts of balance become a part of our everyday rituals and routine which instills a sense of confidence that we can easily take on no matter what the rest of the day throws at us.

DEVELOP A ROUTINE.

I learned the fundamentals of detailed time management from Tony Robbins's RPM System, which taught me to account for all 168 hours in every week through a detailed, tedious process. Every Sunday, during a block of about two to three hours, I would account for all my time that week and plan it on a calendar.

As Tony Robbins says, "If it's not booked, it won't happen."[10] That system saved me weeks of time while allowing me to manage a growing, multinational company and successfully juggling a growing family business. I was also able to build two new real estate projects, all while giving quality time to my wife and three small children while using this system.

Through my time management study, I learned a phrase that I repeat to myself on a daily basis, "Everything can be *done*." My wife laughs at me when I tell her exactly what I'm planning to do two hours before an event, because it's ambitious. But my goals get done. I do what I say I'm going to get done without feeling over-whelmed, because of my ability to compound time, which I picked up from Darren Hardy's book, *The Compound Effect*. His concept of time management has morphed into my lifestyle. Now, I simplify my time by immediately booking all my appointments into my Google Calendar while I'm thinking or talking about them. Time begins to work in your favor when you become a master at deciding to control your choices and priorities.

Every day I work through the steps of my morning routine and don't book any meetings during that time unless there's a real emergency. Nothing gets booked on my calendar before I have time to wake up my kids and feed myself with my resetting ritual and exercise. Without my morning ritual, I don't feel charged to my

---

10   Tony Robbins, "Business Mastery," (live event, Las Vegas, NV, January 2013).

best capacity to take on the day. I know every Legacy Element has to have its micro-balance, each element has to be given attention every day. That means quality time for my family, abundantly leading my organizations, and connecting to my Source, as well as recharging my physical energy and making sure my mind-set is right throughout my day. It's a deep-seeded balance that I honor and cherish. Every morning I wake up and take the time to be grateful for the opportunity to grow my sense of self, as well as my inner legacy champion.

If we develop rituals early during the process of becoming a champion of our legacy, we become the masters of where we dedicate our focus. The discipline and effort of our practice are ultimately what matter, not the balance itself, but the attempt to make our own time as intentional as possible. Successful people understand that part of their power is being in charge of their time and being knowledgeable of where it's being allocated with intention and purpose.

ACTIVELY TAKE BACK YOUR TIME.

Let's get the math out of the way. There are 8,760 hours in a year, 720 hours in a month, and 168 hours in a week. When we think of time, we think of it as an unlimited quantity. Each day blends into the next until we take the concept of time for granted as a commodity that will always be there, available for us to put off and reschedule engagements. But that's not the case. Until we start dissecting our typical week, we don't start realizing how precious time is in our lives, and how much we waste away on time investments of low value. Once we become educated and aware of the value of our time, we will begin to compound time and leverage our activities. That way we can assure ourselves that we're including every Legacy Element that's necessary to have a complete and successful day.

THE DISTRACTION REACTION

By becoming intentional creators versus reacting to outside stimuli such as social media and our phone addictions, we can learn to block out time in a week for the things that we consider important. One way to master our time is by learning to turn off your notifications, sounds, and vibrations on our phones. This easy button press has a significant impact.

Right now, we're wired to respond to a constant barrage of messages, always reacting rather than embracing the present. These distractions create an unnecessary sense of urgency that should be driving us to achieve bigger and better goals in our lives outside of the digital world. Unless a message is crucial to business or family, we can effectively take back our time by ignoring the constant media and retuning our time to work for us. By recreating that balance we allow ourselves to draw back to our centers and remind ourselves of what truly is important beyond outside influences.

Even modern science has coined the "Distraction Reaction" within a social study done by Gloria Mark of the University of California, Irvine, which shows that on average when our brains move from being focused to a distraction it takes our brains up to twenty-five minutes to get back on track. That's a long time when we consider that the average smartphone gets 65.9 notifications a day and that the younger generations invest more than nineteen hours a day in front of screens.[11] Not to mention whenever we engage within the digital world a positive reinforcement response releases serotonin, a micro-chemical in our brain that makes us feel loved and wanted, inevitably forming an addiction to digital communication

---

11   Martin Pilot, Karen Church, and Rodrigo de Oliveira, "An In-Situ Study of Mobile Phone Notifications," accessed June 7, 2018, http://ic.unicamp. br/~oliveira/doc/MHCI2014_An-in-situ-study-of-mobile-phone-notifica-tions.pdf.

and engagement. Once we disengage from that reaction, we can find our own limitless happiness within ourselves.

Be the master of your own life process, not the slave to other people's opinions. You should feel entitled to your own time, not pressured to give it to other people or to things that don't move you forward toward your ultimate goals.

WAYS TO REFOCUS AND TAKE BACK YOUR TIME

If you feel yourself falling into misalignment with your Legacy Elements process or need to activate more healthy ways to use your intentional time, follow these tips:

- Take a moment to be mindful in a quick three-to-five-minute meditation.

- If you have a desk job, take a three-to-five-minute break every thirty to forty-five minutes.

- Knock out your highest leverage item early on in the day.

- I used to have an open-door policy all day when I was working. Now I have daily closed-door times when I'm not bothered and when I can get into a zone, focus, and execute to the best of my ability.

- I use my car as my learning room and listen to audio books and a plethora of other audio-driven content at 1.25x speed to stimulate my thoughts and maximize my drive time. I don't listen to the radio. If I'm not listening to an audiobook or my playlist to get into a certain mind-set, it's quiet, so I can think and be present.

- Read; it's a great way to fall asleep.

- I approach plane rides and work trips as my secluded days

and I love them. I read, sleep, and swim in my thoughts and write all day long. I have playlists that get me into that mind-set almost immediately. I have a song for everything.

- I don't waste time watching TV anymore. Instead I invest in date nights at the movies with my queen.

- I used to be a current events junkie. Now if it's urgent and important enough, it will find me. I do read some business publications and check into news once a week.

- My biggest time waster is watching sports and keeping up with my sports teams.

The problem is that most people say that certain goals are a priority but that they don't have time. Then when we break down their 168 hours of their week that's available to them, they typically find and average fifteen hours per week of wasted time on things they admit aren't a priority or blocks of time they can't even account for during their week. Fifteen hours a week. That's an entire month per year down the drain. What more could you accomplish with a thirteen-month year?

People overestimate what they can do in a month and underestimate what they can do in a year. We must be expectantly precise about our reality before we start discounting what we can or can't do or when letting our own minds create unnecessary drama that distracts us from our usable time. What's your consistency for every Legacy Element? We must find our weakest link within our Legacy Elements and raise it so we can boost and leverage all our others. By identifying our weaknesses in the elements, we can raise our efforts as a whole while dedicating the same amount of time to tasks. The tide raises all boats, and the tide is our commitment to the Legacy Elements.

Ask yourself why you're stuck and what needs to happen to

move forward. Many times, we're alone in our analysis. Our limitations are the pinballs in our brain bouncing off a limited number of examples, opinions, and opportunities. Once we start opening up and being raw with ourselves about achieving our desires, then we start discovering the time, the opportunity, and the resources to shift that reality into place.

TAKING BACK YOUR TIME EXERCISE

Time, when leveraged, will continually add little-by-little to our success. For example, let's do an exercise together to truly gauge whether we're using our time to the best of our abilities every day.

Make a list of your current obligations, tasks, distractions, and the weekly allotment of time you dedicate to them. It's a simple exercise, but be truthful. Put it all out on the table and hold nothing back. By forming a better, more in-depth awareness we'll benefit in the short term as well as in the long run.

Now, how many of those distractions are related to social media, TV, or series watching? How many of them don't impact our business whether through marketing or research? I think we'll find that useless social media takes up a majority of our time, and can take a backseat to our actual intentions to live a healthier, less-distracted life. We become driven by external factors instead of mastering our internal understanding of who we want to be in this life. This chasing ultimately leaves us spinning our wheels and unsure of how to reach our goals or form a true legacy.

Time is a concept that can only serve you if you make the effort to understand as well as maximize each moment to the best of your ability. By minimizing distractions and creating a cultivated awareness of where your energy needs to be invested to impact your legacy, you can truly strive to be your best self without anyone else's interruptions weighing you down. Every action you take toward maintaining balance in your life echoes through your future choices, ensuring that when times grow tough you'll have a basis for consistency that will keep you firm in your convictions as a legacy champion. You'll be better equipped to create your legacy by transcending the past, ruling your legacy by balancing the present, and expanding your legacy by serving future generations.

Finally, remember where you are. I am forty-two; the average US male lives seventy-nine years. That leaves me thirty-seven years, less than half of what I've already lived to make my remaining dreams true. But not even those seventy-nine are guaranteed. So, if I'm taking this seriously and with responsibility, I better get moving. How much time do you have left?

BRINGING YOUR LEGACY FULL CIRCLE

In the end, the parking brakes of life are always present and must be consciously transcended as we move onto our next learning experience of ourselves.

I once was filled with fear. Fear of failing, fear of my identity being crushed, fear of my petty, ego-driven metrics. Now I love myself, forgive myself, motivate myself, and build myself up like a young boy playing his first games. I know that I must hustle and learn from my mistakes with a sense of urgency rivaled only by my will to remain aware at all time. I must keep on trying and not be ashamed of seeking help or asking questions to move forward on the path I've laid out for myself. My coaches are everywhere I turn, I only have to look, listen, and acknowledge life's teachable moments. My intentional passion must be ever present, and as time passes, focus becomes attainable and maturity condenses into the tranquility and happiness of a man on a mission. I must never stop serving others or myself through embracing my overarching awareness of the life I've been given and the power I hold in my hands to mold it.

This mission is one of gratitude, service, and never-ending improvement, always striving for something better, but at the same time being content with the day's labors and advancements. While we always look forward, we should also always strive to appreciate whatever the present provides for us. Make your case and let your spirit run, let it drive you, pull you, and intrigue you into the greater expanse of your own inner unknown where every day becomes clearer. Our power manifests itself through our growing awareness as we come into our own as people, family, significant others, entrepreneurs, and human beings.

Our power is our internal belief in ourselves. Leadership requires discipline, courage, and taking the risk of being vulnerable. These acts require focus, presence, and effort, because they're not a natural state in humans. Therefore, we can get easily burnt out while trying to execute them. So, to feed and nurture ourselves as leaders, we need to take breaks and reconnect with ourselves, to our purpose, through reflection, contemplation, connection with other leaders, and reenergizing the commitment to our goals, which isn't a once and done thing.

How often are you feeding and nurturing yourself to assure that your commitment is certain? As one of my mentors tells me, "Uncertainty is the obligation without the commitment." By restoring your faith in your inner certainty, you're building up your leadership capabilities. From experience, I can say that it is much more beneficial, productive, and lucrative to operate your legacy from a position of certainty.

Now that you've navigated your way through the path you need to walk to champion your legacy, with your knowledge you should:

- have a clear dashboard of the Legacy Elements that comprise becoming a legacy champion

- How to measure these six Legacy Elements

- How to balance them in a daily basis as well as through the long-term.

Regardless of where you began this journey, as well as this book, you should have a gained a better understanding that your future as a legacy champion will only be limited by your weakest Legacy Element(s). So it behooves you to work on each element with individual and focused clarity. By keeping your end goals in sight and nurturing your Legacy Elements, you'll be able to prepare for future tunnels you will encounter and how to quickly step out of them with a sense of expanded legacy and a stronger internal certainty.

Through these pages you've learned creation and legacy mastery. Now is truly when the journey to becoming a legacy champion begins because we have to take the pieces that we've learned to expand past our minds into constant iterations and tireless improvement to keep our Legacy Elements working for ourselves.

"Every day do something that makes you sweat, every week do something that makes you hurt, and every month do something that scares the hell out of you!" is a favorite quote of mine by Ben Greenfield, a recognized fitness coach, whose premise I utilize on a daily basis. As a barometer, keep these questions in mind throughout your continued growth in the process:

- What scares you?

- Which of those fears are holding you back from happiness or a sense of peace?

- What are your regrets?

Recognizing our regrets becomes an undeniable byproduct of the legacy champion process, purely because confronting those regrets will allow us to come face to face with the truth of whether we're flexible and willing to make the choice to continue our expansion—for our benefit as well as to provide a solid example for those around us.

This book is to serve as your stepping stone for expanding an indestructible legacy. What you do with your next steps on the path is within your power to determine, but only your continued awareness of your legacy impact can shift regrets to restoration, molding yourself into an ultimate legacy champion.

Welcome to your journey. Enjoy the ride.

LEGACY ELEMENTS
ASSESSMENT TOOLKIT

Assess your current state in the six LEGACY Elements. On a scale of 0-100 percent, at what capacity and alignment are you currently operating in each element, in regard to what you are capable of or desire? (20 percent—very low capacity; 100 percent—very high capacity).

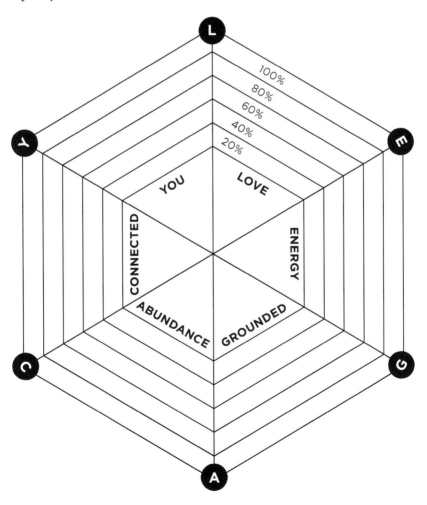

Legacy Elements for improvement are those in which you have rated yourself less than 80 percent.

Write the Elements needing improvement in order of priority:

1. _____

_____

_____

_____

_____

2. _____

_____

_____

_____

_____

3. _____

_____

_____

_____

_____

4. _____

_____

_____

_____

_____

_____

5. _____

_____

_____

_____

_____

_____

6. _____

_____

_____

_____

_____

_____

ACKNOWLEDGEMENTS

I'd like to thank my wife, Marcela, who has supported me in my projects and has been a voice of reason, practicality, and simplicity with many of my ideas. She has given me much of the content in this book through our experiences and challenges. She has supported and refined me every step of the way. She has shown me what unconditional giving is to others and intentionally has helped me to create the most important venture: family. For your love, patience, and support, thank you, Amor!

To my children Gian Carlo, Alexia Maria, and Marcel Alessandro, the three of you are why I do what I do. You fulfill me with so much motivation, happiness, and fun that it is hard to imagine a lifestyle with you as adults. I hope to continue being a loving and passionate father for you and to help guide you through this adventure of life. For the rest of days, thank you and I love you!

Mom, you have been a guiding light of love and support since the beginning. You helped spawn my spiritual journey within. Your unconditional love and support has been the best cheerleading anyone can ask for. I'm the luckiest son in the world to have your infinite presence rooting for me every day no matter the distance or time between us. Thank you for all your gifts!

Dad, I know you are with me every step of the way and I feel your presence. Thank you for always taking care of me and demanding my best results. Your legacy runs through me and I do my best to honor your true spirit!

To Lucia and Alex, thank you for being such awesome siblings and business partners. I value our challenges and collaborations to be great learning experiences. Thank you for your trust and support to allow me to develop myself as a leader, in our organizations and family.

To Nando, Gabe, and Bernardo, thank you for your support in different stages of my life when I needed additional support and guidance, you were there for me.

To Ernesto Cutie, whose friendship and trust is that of a lifetime. To have a brother from another family is a reality; thank you for a lifetime of support and friendship.

Thank you to my friends, business partners, and forum mates who have joined me on my path and supported me along the way: Ricardo Teran, Rodrigo Mantica, Guillermo Groisman, Markus Ros, Joao Mucciolo, Arnoldo Poncon, Flemming Lund, Erick Holmann, Pedro Alvarez, Ricardo Melendez, Diego Vargas, Piero Coen, Horacio Rappaccioli, Max Garcia, Gian Innocenti, Rodrigo Zamora, and Ernesto Baltodano. Your standards, leadership, and experiences have allowed me to be a much more complete person; I hope to make all of you proud.

Thank you to my coaches and mentors of recent years: Jose Bolaños, Darin Rowell, and Raul Villacis. Your ability to get me uncomfortable has allowed me to grow in so many ways. Thank you to my brothers in the EDGE brotherhood, who allow me the space to be completely real. A special thank you to Bob Gallo, Juan Carlos Garcia, Jason Bledsoe, and Joe Schirmer.

Thank you to those organizations which have helped form me and truly have a special place in my heart: Aspen Institute, Entrepreneurs' Organization, and YPO. Your impact on leaders and entrepreneurs is so profound and has been life changing for me, thank you.

Thank you to my other coaches and mentors and authors, some of whom I've met and others I never will. Your impact on me has been important and lasting. Thank you for your sacrifice, dedication, and gifts to the world! Anthony Robbins, Darren Hardy, Jim Rohn, Brian Johnson, Wayne Dyer, Keith Cunningham, Napoleon Hill, Eckhart Tolle.

To my friends at Advantage Media Group|ForbesBooks who helped guide me in this first go around: Alison, Justin, Carly, and especially Elise and Eland. You all have been instrumental in helping me refine the delivery of my ideas and this book. It has been both a pleasure and fun working with you, thank you!

Thank you, Jose Menendez, your help to deliver my message to the world is greatly appreciated and I enjoy working with you.

Thank you to all the team members who have ever joined and supported my visions. Thank you for your time and effort to make my visions a reality for so many. You have challenged me and allowed me to grow while on your time. I hope that your time with me is memorable and worthwhile.

To all my friends and family who have supported me to go forward to make my dreams a reality, I thank you. Every comment of moral support and question of interest is important fuel to take the next step forward.

Finally, I'd like to acknowledge all the entrepreneurs out there who work hard to sacrifice their peace of mind and family nest eggs and put themselves last on the list when it is needed. You are the breed that this world needs aligned with universal values to right our course and make sure that the legacy of our generation is one of great importance for all mankind.

ABOUT THE AUTHOR

Gian Marco is the president of CASCO Safety Group (Central America Safety Company), Central America's leading distributor of specialized industrial safety and rescue equipment. He is the president of Café Las Flores, Nicaragua's finest coffee company and leading integrated specialty coffee brand from plantation to retail. He is also present in the commercial real estate development space with Centro Norte and Entheos Centro Corporativo, both in Managua.

He promotes responsible business practices as a board member of uniRSE, Nicaragua's CSR catalyst. Current and past board positions include Fundacion Cocibolca and Paso Pacifico, two of Nicaragua's leading biodiversity and environmental actors. Gian Marco is a CALI (Central American Leadership Initiative) Fellow from the Aspen Institute and part of the Aspen Global Leadership Initiative. He was named to the BMW Foundation's inaugural class of Latin American Young Leaders Forum.

He graduated from the Georgia Institute of Technology in Atlanta, Georgia, in 1997. Since then, he has graduated from Entrepreneurs' Organization's EO/MIT Entrepreneurial Masters Program, multiple INCAE executive programs, and Anthony Robbins' Mastery University. He was the first speaker in the inaugural TEDx Managua event in 2012.

His investment in personal development covers two decades and he loves to coach, mentor and interact with other entrepreneurs. Gian Marco is an active member of Entrepreneurs' Organization (EO), and a founding member of the YPO Nicaragua Chapter, where he takes active leadership roles.

Gian Marco loves to read, write, travel, play and follow sports, and invest in quality family time. He currently resides in Managua with his wife Marcela and three children.

OUR SERVICES

If you are interested in developing your legacy more in depth and with continued support, we recommend looking at our additional resources:

LEGACY CREATION RESOURCE

At Legacy Lifestyle, we help others accelerate their personal and business growth so they can start achieving more towards their legacy creation. Our website, http://gmpalazio.com/, serves as a resource hub to learn more about how to create, rule, and expand your legacy.

LEGACY COMMUNITY

If you want to advance with living your legacy day by day, join our Rule Your Legacy Facebook group and be part of an interactive community supported by like-minded leaders and guided by Gian Marco. Members are helped to fine-tune their approach to legacy creation. Group members will gain useful insights on multiplying their Legacy through a series of exclusive live broadcast sessions and Q&A's with Gian Marco. To join simply go to facebook.com/gmpalazio and click on the 'Groups' tab.

LEGACY ELEMENT ASSESSMENT TOOLKIT

Our toolkit helps you identify your current deficiencies within the legacy diamond. The assessment provides an understanding based on a proven roadmap to help you achieve your personal best. From practical tools to accomplish your dreams and goals, to clearing an intentional path to greater influence and contribution, our toolkit gives you a customizable startup and intermediary roadmap. Watch the instructional video and get access to the assessment download link: http://gmpalazio.com/legacy-assessment-toolkit.

LEGACY LIFESTYLE ACADEMY

This work study course is designed to help you situationally tackle all areas of life needing improvement to create clarity, alignment, and take action to change your life. Learn how to multiply legacy as a business leader, husband, father, community supporter, and citizen of the world. The course will be made up of key lessons formatted in video and audio with monthly downloadable course content. In addition, Gian Marco will mentor group participants by hosting frequent live sessions with academy participants to provide relevant, timely, practical solutions to tackle common group challenges. Learn more at the following link: http://gmpalazio.com/legacy-lifestyle-academy.

LEGACY MASTERY EVENT

This is a live event for anyone seeking coaching and support to achieve their greatest legacy in this lifetime. If your life seems off track and you're struggling to achieve your legacy dreams and can't figure things out, this is the place to get back on course and gain measurable results so you can stop inertia and start living your legacy. Being challenged by obstacles is normal, but getting stuck doesn't have to be inescapable. The Legacy Mastery Event is designed to provide one-on-one feedback and real-world solutions through my personal coaching so you can get on a fast track to legacy creation and start living the life of your dreams. Learn more: http://gmpalazio. com/legacy-mastery-event.

SPEAKING ENGAGEMENTS

If you're interested in scheduling Gian Marco to speak at your company meeting, conference, or convention, please contact: support@ gmpalazio.com.

LEGACY INSPIRATION QUOTES

https://www.instagram.com/gmpalazio/

Printed in the USA
CPSIA information can be obtained
at www.ICGtesting.com
JSHW012031140824
68134JS00033B/2994